Under The Hill

BY JOHN FORSTER

Published by
John Forster
Wotton-under-Edge,
Gloucestershire, GL12 7LY

© John Forster

Printed 2005

ISBN: 0-955 1103-0-0

Printed and Bound in Great Britain by
Woolnough Bookbinding, Irthlingborough, Northants.

DEDICATION

To my dear wife, Pat,
a great stalwart.

ACKNOWLEDGEMENTS

I am grateful to Mrs Christine Fulton for allowing me to use her article describing the effects of foot and mouth at her brothers' farm; and also to Mrs Rosamond Smith for her graphic letter telling a similar story on their farm.

CONTENTS

TO THE HUSBANDMAN

Thou husbandman, that faire wouldst know
Some remedies to finde;
How for to helpe thy sickly beast;
To satisfy thy minde:
Here mayst thou learne plentie thereof,
Thou needst not further to go:
But therein search, and thou shalt finde
Such helpes to helpe their woe:
And when thou wouldst fairre cattell keepe,
For to maintaine the stocke:
Thou must learne as well the helpes
As to increase thy stocke.
For if thou seekest first the beast,
And knowest not how to use him:
When he fal'th sicke, alwaies thou art
In danger to lose him.
For want of knowledge and good skill
Oft times it may so fall:
A man that is full rich in beastes,
He may soone lose them all.
Therefore in this counsell thee,
Seeke first to help disease:
As great a praise to him that saves,
As he that can increase.

Leonard Mascall
The First Booke of Cattell (1605)

v

ABOUT THIS BOOK

This is the true story of two places –
a corner of Gloucestershire; and another corner in Wales.

Both of these corners become joined by the experiences of
an English breeder of Welsh cattle.

AUTHOR

John Forster was born in Bristol in 1939, the second son of a Gloucestershire mother and North country father.

After leaving school he worked for a short time as a clerk with an animal feed company.

He spent the following years, from his late teens until mid twenties on Gloucestershire dairy farms, with a break at the County Farm Institute.

Going self-employed into poultry keeping, ("the cheapest way to get into farming"), he produced brown eggs – ("which the public wanted, at a time when most producers were producing white eggs - which the public didn't want").

At about this time he married Pat, ("thank goodness"), and later was able to get back to his favourite farm animal – the cow – which he breeds and rears on a part-time basis. ("Most certainly not hobbying though – they have to pay bills").

He has two sons, ("well and truly grown up, and successfully dissuaded from farming – you either have to be mad, or have your heart where your brain should be to do farming").

AUTHOR'S NOTE

Everything here, in this book, is true, except, of course, the dream, but the dream, even so is told exactly as it unfolded before me on that night. And it was the dream, which after years of pondering, persuaded me to write down those things, which have remained locked in my mind for so long.

Every place here is real – some so real that they are indelibly imprinted on my brain. The characters are real; some have their own names, others have fictitious names, depending on how I considered them. Because, of course, there are those who are the salt of the earth and those who I feel should just be named for reasons that will be obvious Each and every event took place; some were really happy - and many were unforgettably sad.

All the animals were there. Many are still here. They all have minds and emotions, which, in turn, have a tremendous bearing on ours. Nature, to those who work amongst it, is a difficult thing to explain to those who don't. Perhaps, in a small way, a whiff of that mystery might be sensed in these pages.

Nothing is without its irritations, and if anything, those things written here that appear closest to fiction really must be taken as fact, for they are the splatter dash and posturing of civil servants, and mindless politicians of our own- and just as if we didn't have enough of them, there are those across the Channel as well.

Don't underestimate their power.

Despite all the failings, I am immensely grateful to have spent so much time 'tied to a cow's tail' because it is these spin-offs that have made it all so worthwhile and enjoyable.

CHAPTER 1

The Dream

"You've got some fine Galloway cattle up there on the hill" a newly arrived in-comer remarked to me one day. Needless to say I took him to one side and corrected him.

Why is it, I always ask myself does everyone seem to know about Galloways and Belted Galloways, and yet so few people have heard of the Welsh cattle, which by some strange freak of nature have the same markings and colours.

Galloway is about 200 miles by sea from the northern – most tip of Wales, and yet here we have, in these two places, native cattle which look identical. Both breeds have a pre-dominance of black cattle but both, by some strange mystery also have other colours too, such as belted, white, red, smoky and line-backed. No one has ever been able to explain this despite attempts to trace both breeds ancestry. Ancient manuscripts and documents record cattle bearing the different colours in both places.

All anyone will say is: "That it must have always been this way."

Although colours and markings make animals look identical, to those who keep these beasts the differences are obvious. The Welsh cattle tend to be heavier and thicker, with larger, friendlier heads; they grow horns whereas their Scottish cousins do not and the general feeling in Wales is that their cattle are more docile and placid, thus making them easier to handle.

Whether it was on this particular evening I had been pondering these unsolved questions which must have puzzled countless other breeders of those animals down the ages, I cannot recall; but I do know that on that night I had a dream which was so vivid I was able to relate every bit of its detail to my wife on the following morning.

Although in the cold light and logic of day the dream did seem rather unlikely. I do, just the same think we are generally just a little quick to dismiss those things which we do not always fully understand.

Nevertheless, I will tell the dream as it unfolded before me on that night: and leave you to judge.

It was not far from the beginning of time when there were bad tempered, wild black cattle in the south west of Scotland, which those who lived there tried to tame with little success. There were at that time too, just a few amongst these cattle who didn't much care for all this wildness, all this bad temper, and all this heavy fighting. It was they who took themselves away and grazed in contentment and peacefulness by themselves.

As the years passed, there were still only a few of these quiet beasts, three or four dozen black cows and their calves, and a handful of very quiet and well-behaved bulls. There were too, by now just a small number of the other colours, who had the same peaceful nature, and had come along and gently joined the rest.

Galloway, for that is what we now call where they lived, is a pleasant place, hilly, watered in plenty, and green to look upon. Mild by the kindness by the passing of those soft seas and airs which touch its shores and fill its skies as they pass by on their journey from the south. This friendly warmness during those days was only known for what it was; never did anyone have a name for it, only now do we call it the Gulf Stream.

Although near the shores of this place all was pleasant and kind; there were many high hilly places away from it where the wind and the winters were heavy on the mind and body. Places where cattle needed to be strong and hardy. Places where cattle, when the days grew short, and the coldness gripped their frames would have to have a great strength to survive, and it was those that were born without this strength, which soon perished; for nature at her worst is cruel, and has no regard for them which are the unfortunate weak.

So for many years, the placid black cows of Galloway lived, and were tolerated by their more wild cousins: but this land, being what it is; as time moved, the numbers of the wild grew greater, and the placid beasts found that they were increasingly struggling for pasture against the aggression of the others.

Whether by crafty design, or whether by accident, the placid black beasts, over time found themselves getting closer and closer to the west side of that place. Now you will recall that the part of Galloway to the west is also closest to the sea where it is warmest, and because of this grows the best grass, so it would be unlikely that the placid would be allowed by the wild to move here out of choice. Nevertheless, that is where they found themselves; but that was not to remain the case for long.

It was, on a night in the spring of that year, when the moon was bright behind the flitting clouds, and the placid beasts were settling to their night's rest, feeling contented with the new grass in their bellies, which was beginning to show itself all emerald green in the pastureland about them; that the dark hillside against where they were settled began to stir, and a movement could be sensed by the pale whiteness of the moon.

3

For those who have never kept black cattle, it might seem that a man could always see his stock if he were close enough to them, even in deadest of night. But I have passed within three yards, of two dozen sleeping beasts and not known them to be there. That is how it was, on that fateful night. Only could the dullest thud of many hooves on the turf be heard against the soft lapping of the gentle sea: only the pushing of branches, and the rustle of bushes told your senses that somewhere very near was a great force bearing down on that quiet spot where those gentle cattle were deep within their sleep. In the whole of that place about them there was movement; a movement like stealth, slowly getting closer, but only did it still remain a sound: gentle but vast: all about: although nowhere could be seen anything that moved.

It is a soft sound that will often make us wake if we are not used to hearing it, even if we will sleep through heavy noise, for it is what our minds are used to which is where the difference lies: and it is not just us humans who are like this, for animals have this help too.

Those about the outside of the sleeping herd were the first to move their heads from their sides; for that is the way of cattle when they lie in the deepness of sleep. Almost the way of a cat, although the stiffness of their hard frames will always prevent them from gathering themselves into the closeness of a ball as a cat might. Those that had first stirred, looked hard with tension towards where the sounds were stealing. Whilst their eyes told them nothing, their ears spoke earnestly to them, as at that same moment, did their twitching noses. Slowly they rose to their feet, for although they had never before had this experience, the softness of the sounds all about them showed for them yet, no fear. Where they were, they stood; gradually having the rest, heaving their great black woolly frames from the flattened grass of their sleep, and too, standing there looking with what might just as well have been blinded eyes into the misted greys and blacks of the moonlit moor. Yet, their big ears, still with that thickness of winter coat

4

about them, cocked and sharpened to the growing sounds, and their wide black wet noses set deep, with nostrils twitching gently for the slightest whiff of what was all about, that slowly told them the realisation of what was there, —was not right.

By now the calves, from sense learned through birth, and taught by dam, were on their feet, had stretched away their sleep, and high alert was in their stance; the tenseness of the moment was soon within them too.

The herd, complete, and standing motionless and silent looked searchingly, not believing that so many muffled feet could now be on three sides of them, and yet, no sight was seen, save just the silhouette of the trees and hilltop against the clear starred sky. The scent of others now wafted on the still night air from those three sides where all the sound was coming. Our leader cast her head high now, to test the air for other smells that might be there to comfort her from those she took to be a threat. The only thread of air that showed that comfort for which she searched, was from her fourth side, and away from the dulled thud of those hooves. That scent she had known all her long years; that taste of salt it bore, as well as its freshness. But from where it came had always been strange to her, for it appeared an endless space, so flat and smooth, with gentle lapping noises all about it, quite different from the grassy hills and slopes which stood each day the same. For too, that strange place could change its shape from the flat, endless, noiseless plain to roaring mountains, moving high into the heavens, a shocking sight to see. But this night, once more, that place was as a flat plain, motionless in the pale light.

Soon the leader turned towards this direction, and made to go that way, for there being no other choice, she was left with little to decide about her herd's fate. The rest quickly followed knowing this too. Slowly but deliberately they walked gently down the soft grassy slope towards the lapping water's edge. The calves, who normally skipped danced and raced each other in the expectation of new pastures whenever their dams moved off, were not so inclined to that tonight, they were calm and quiet as they are when their forms and minds are troubled with sickness, not even this time did they trot to be the first to take the new fresh grass, but followed obediently behind.

A coldness struck the leaders nose as she lowered her head to smell the moving water at her feet, but never did she attempt to taste, for she had only done this once, and that in her youth. Not here the soft flavour of the mountain stream which cooled her dry mouth in the long hot summer days. But here was foul, trenchant stuff, which caused the tongue to crave the freshness of the waters on the hillside.

Momentarily she paused to gaze out across the expanse before her, for never had she, or all those she had ever known, been past this place. As she stood; soon the others following, gathered behind her, silently waiting for what next was to happen, and when the last calf arrived and stood motionless with the rest, she looked round, gathering them all into her sight: and I know this, and no one will persuade me otherwise, that cows do weep; for I have seen it many times before, when sadness beholds them, at the times when a new-born calf gives up the struggle for life because of some illness that has gripped it, and the sorrow in the mother becomes great, as great as that of a man's wife if ever she should lose her child.

As if she knew in her depth of feeling that what she was about to do, would lead her, and those who stood motionless beside her, and with all their trust held tight against her, to a fate from which they might never return, for if that vastness before them, was by experience like its taste, they would surely go on to a most terrible end.

Slowly but deliberately her heavy thick feet stepped into the gently lapping water as it played about the sand on the beach, the coldness meant nothing to her, neither the wet, for it was always about them, with so much stormy weather in that country. Soon, as she moved on, the waters were to her hocks, and those who she led began to follow obediently behind; they too were now no more on dry land, but amongst the vastness of that great space and, which by now began to take more and more of their big woolly frames from sight as into its depth they went, until its enormous strength began lifting their heavy bodies from the firmness of the floor beneath them, and the softly flowing waters began carrying them away, out, out, into the moonlit desert, stretching endlessly on. Then, as the eye strained in the watching of that hopeless little party, becoming smaller and smaller, as the distance from the shore grew greater; no longer could any shape or form be made out, not even that of the last little calf; but only the flatness and silence of that which had borne them away from the land that had been their home for so long.

CHAPTER 2

Solitude

If there ever was a place that God, when he created the earth intended men to settle; a place where they would have endless supplies of fresh water from off the mountains to drink and water their pastures; a place where the wind from the closeness of the sea to the west, and the roughness of the earth to the east was halted by the vastness of the mountains around it. That place would be Dolgellau.

All about that little Welsh town, lying against the foot of Cader Idris in that happy county of Merioneth, are the emerald greens of its tidy little fields, trimmed with huge bouldered walls, stretching their way over the rolling slopes, up, up, to be swallowed by the rocks and heathers of the mountains. If a man needed to take himself out of the care and strife of a day, it is here, on a summer's evening, he should bring himself, to sit on the bank of the River Wnion, as the gentle mists rise up from the heavy grey stones of the buildings, and over their soft blue roofs, to drift across the solid thick chimneys of the town, and away into the woods beyond.

Here it is he can sit quietly and fill his mind with the beauty and calm; here it is, his eye can stretch across the water meadows; up through the wooded slopes, the rough acreages of mountain pastures, and onto the rocky tops of the skyline; and as he runs his gaze along that line, it will stop on the uppermost level, at the saddle of the Cader. It is here his mind will dwell as the evening light fades; until from his sight, it will faintly pass away, and as he turns to make his way back home, he will know that his mind has rested that night, up there on Cader.

It must have been, that those poor unwanted creatures, who found themselves cast into that great ocean in my dream, all those years before near when our time began, knew by their instinct, and surely with God's help, of this place. How, or what price in time and suffering they paid, no man will ever know. But it is, if we look more closely into those tidy green pastures, and over those steep rough slopes on the hillside, we will see amongst the white mountain sheep, their dark black forms quietly grazing. Never could a man tell what their forebears must have experienced, but it must have been of such greatness, as despite all the years that have since passed, it would still remain in the deepness of the minds of those who are here now: and if that were so, they are clever to hide it from us; for they seem at such peace in this gentle place.

If a man cares to walk instead of ride, and if, when he walks, he takes some time to stop and look. For if he is not prepared to do this in these parts, then he has no place here, and he should take himself away instead, with those who draw their pleasures from what is temporary and hollow, and noisy and brash. But if he can see with his eyes what really is before him, then, it is here he will always want to be.

It was at a time when I was many years younger than I am now, that I first met this place. An uncle of my wife had taken a farm in the mountains near Cader. Our journey from where we lived in Gloucestershire took the better part of the day, although many would have done it in less than half that time, but then, they would never have had the pleasures that we had found as we travelled on through this enchanting scenery which stretched out before us along our way.

The beginning of the evening had arrived as we made our way across Eldon Square in Dolgellau, and out again through a tiny twisting narrow street with high grey stone buildings on either side. Never would a man realise how that ordinary little street could lead onto such a place of unforgettable splendour.

Within a short while we were moving from the town; and the road began its sharp climb through the trees and then winding on between bouldered walls out amongst the lushness of the green landscape. As the mist rose on the damp warm summer air, the valley opened its way before us. In its end was the last brightness of the day's sky; and in its nearness to us, the slopes that rose gently up beside our little road enfolded us in all its beauty. Above the tiny fields the boulders scattered across the mountain side showed grey and unreal amongst the greenness of the grass. But in all this roughness of the higher places, the tall boundary walls still strove onwards, up the steep sides, as straight as any rule they went, until, unexhausted, they reached the summit, and not yet beaten, strode on across the skyline, to mark with hardness this farm's land from that of those on the other side of its mountain. Wales has its mountains scored with endless heavy rock walls; set there in those hard years of the 19th century by men who often toiled amongst the slate quarries during their day, and then, by hoping to make a better life, shaping a farm at night, clearing the land they had claimed of its rocks, to make pastures for their flocks and herds, and walls beside which they might keep them.

With still several miles to go, the little road began to have the feel of wildness with the patches of closely cropped grass growing within its middle. All about, the calmness of the mountains began to heave their greatness over us, as the road cut its way grasping at the steep screed slope. On the opposite side of the narrow valley was, amongst a handful of well blown pines and a few brave ash trees, a crouched little farm house, with its grey buildings, seemingly huddled about it for warmth in a hollow which could only have been formed for when a man might pass this way and come and want to live somewhere here. From its tiny square windows a soft patch of light whispered, but this was soon left behind, as the road rose gently, and we clattered over a second cattle grid, and from then on we would have the slowness of opening and closing six gates.

After the first gate; quite suddenly, we were no more in the narrow valley, but a wide open plain, for we had climbed a considerable amount since leaving the town, and the mountain had chased away from our side and rushed ahead of us into the south, and the openness to the north was vast, for the distant mountains seemed to play along the bottom of the fading sky. At this place in the road a rough track forked to our left and took itself off, bolting as hare might, in a straight line, chasing southward after the disappearing mountain. In all its boldness, this track could only have been hacked across so crude and wild a landscape by a Roman, but as time took hold of it, and stole away the harshness of its use from under a thousand soldiers tramping feet, to later give it up to drovers and their herds of placid, gentle black beasts, on their long journey across Wales and England, to feed the hungry mouths of the people in cities, who never would have dreamed of a place such as this, from which their good food could have come.

When a man's thoughts take him back through time, because the place where he is standing causes him to do this; then that place will always hold for him the magic and mystery of its history. Even an old house will often have this presence, and will capture the mind, and set it about its imagination. Is it, perhaps because something of us lives on in a place long after we have departed this earth? All I know is that at this spot where that rough track leaves the road, there is, for me an overbearing sense of the deepness of history stretching back away from us.

Our road, from this point crossed the wide high plain, taking its twisting way through the tired wooden gates which relied as much on the road as they did their hinge for support. After the third gate the road turned suddenly and sharply to the right and dropped from us but we were to stay where we were, and push our way straight on through a fourth gate. From here it climbed sharply for a short time, and made its way between steep high rock faces as if entering a secret place. At its pitch that secret place unfolded before us, and there lay another plain, with the southward chasing mountains joining us once again from the east; and across the plain to the west was our first glimpse of the sea.

As the day was almost gone, we were unable to grasp then how much of that places beauty the fading light hid from us. Perhaps too, we were just beginning to be anxious in wondering where the end of the little road, and our uncle's house would be. Then, as the road slid down, twisting about itself into the plain, there, within half a mile, suddenly, could be seen the whiteness of a light, as if to beckon us across the last piece of that strange and wonderful landscape. Ever since then as long ago as it was, that light still holds for me the same comfort, when we return, as it did on that very first night.

The last warmth of the day still lay with the strips of tarred road either side of the short grass in its middle, and as the lights of the car fell ahead of us, the sheep, with their lambs scuttled away into the darkness on either side, expecting not to be disturbed at this late hour from their sleep on the warm road. After dragging two more gates, and the twisting and dipping of the road, our journey had reached its end. In the fading light, the long low farmhouse now stood against us, with timeless strength drawn from its bouldered walls, and welcoming tiny windows folded between its crevices.

Soon we were in, fed and satisfied. What remained of that day was now only but a dim memory, for my head was still full of the sights we had just lived and I rode that Journey over and over again in my mind, and later took it with me to my bed, where once more; but with all the extra vividness of a dream, I spent the night, not in that darkened room, but along that magical mountain road.

The best surprises come from where we least expect them, or perhaps where we hadn't noticed they could ever be. Never had our eyes fully recognised, as we came to that house, what was all about us in the fading light of the night before. For there, that next day, through the tiny low open bedroom window, was set before us, in the early morning summer sunshine, a sight which I knew then, would go with me for the rest of my life.

Our uncle's farm was settled half way up the mountain side, and looked north west across the 24 miles beyond Barmouth Bay to the Lleyn Peninsula. The turquoise smoothed sea reflected back the clear blue of the morning sky, where at its greatest distance it touched the dusky purple mountains of the Lleyn. The silver beaches of Merionethshire drifted gently down and the eye was drawn back along the coast again, to rest on what, from our height looked like a fairy-tale town across the estuary beneath.

Here, as with us, all seemed peaceful and calm, but distance can be a great deceiver, for the town of Barmouth could never be described as any of this, although, like most of life, even the bad has its good side, and over the years I have grown to enjoy Barmouth, its distant views, crowded streets, derelict empty buildings, the hurly burly of the fairgrounds, the wide stretches of soft white sand, tall grey Victorian piles which used to serve as seaside boarding houses for droves of Liverpudlian holiday makers, who spewed from crowded trains arriving at the station during the peak weeks of the summer season, when the industrial north closed down, and the holiday towns of the Welsh coast came to life.

Nowhere is free from change, the hoards go off to Spain instead now, and the trains arrive like cut-down excuses of their forebears. Black smoke is replaced by a faint blue hue; angry hissing steam, and roaring fires as the packed carriages were dragged gliding along; has given way to the gentle hum and honking horn of half empty funny buses. They arrive by car now, and don't stay in the boarding houses, but go up the coast to the vast caravan sites looking like council estates, where they feel more at home; and where there aren't any landladies telling them what time to come in at night, or when to get down for breakfast in the morning.

So, when the sun touches the end of Ceredigion Bay, and the streets of Barmouth become deserted, and we turn back along the harbour to the edge of the town, where there is a narrow little opening, and a footpath. It can all still be left behind once more. Here is the place where a man can take a step from one sort of life, where there is noise and crowds and clamour, to another, where there is peace and solitude and beauty. A place where the saltiness of the sea reaches through, under the piers of Barmouth bridge to touch the quiet still pure waters of the Mawddach Estuary. A place where the mountains stand guard over that far bank, protecting its stillness from the hustle and bustle of the other side. And as a man enjoys the company of his wife, as he shares this beauty with her, and each is drawn closer to the other as they walk along the pathway of life; so, as they walk along that narrow wooden path of the railway bridge, do they draw closer to that beauty on the far bank. But as they reach that bank, and look back, once more they will feel sure that that which they have just left is itself all peace and stillness; for distance remains the great deceiver; and the noise of that place will never span that stretch of water to pollute the other side; and always, from our uncle's farm will that special view hold its magical charm, with the turquoise sea, the purple mountains, and the fairy-tale town.

CHAPTER 3

Unless You Had Been There – How Would You Know?

Pedigree sales of Welsh cattle generally take place away from the summer, probably because everyone is too busy then to bother with the fussing of their beasts to make them look their best for selling. There sometimes are those who try to practise slight of eye, and this can happen with all types of livestock besides just cattle.

Although a visit to an agricultural show is always an enjoyable way to spend a summer's day; one place at a show I never enjoy so much are the livestock sheds. How fully grown, tough looking men bring themselves to spend two or three days clipping and shampooing-and-setting their charges hair, I find hard to understand. Trying to turn an ordinary looking beast into a film star is a great talent which some are very skilled at; and by the time they have finished with the clippers and combs, a normal looking animal becomes a big square, deep-chested, wide rumped, body builder. What surprises me even more though, is that the judges appear to be fooled by it all. I call it deceitful, and wish it could be stopped. As long as they are clean and tidy, that should be enough for all of us. How to prevent the filling up of an animal's belly with cake to make him grow faster would be a more difficult task to deal with though. Many a man has taken home a big well- grown young bull from a sale, feeling all proudness within him for paying the top price of the day; to find after a few weeks of feeding him just good grass or best hay or silage, that he melts before him like a chocolate bar beside the fire. The beast was grown too soon on lots of very expensive food, which an ordinary farmer could never afford to be always feeding.

It must be a wise man who looks beyond what he sees in the pen or ring, to the history of the beast, and the credibility of its owners; for that is where the promise lies.

The star performers in the sale or show rings are very often the lady breeders; generally the ones who are doing it for a hobby, those who are not depending on a good sale to provide the children with some new shoes or clothes; or to get the roof on their windswept farmhouse mended, because it is becoming too expensive to keep buying all those buckets. These are the ladies who, when they have finished hairdressing their cattle, and an hour before the lorry is due to leave the farm for the sale, go off themselves, down to the town, and have their own hair dressed. How they manage to balance keeping both lots of hair in place long enough to get to the end of the sale, is a trick which must be worth learning. It is these ladies; who are not found at the sales in the wilder places, but more in England, and the softer parts of West Wales.

At the Llandovery pedigree sale one such middle-aged lady puts in an appearance most years. Her husband assists her in the driving of each of her animals from the pens to the sale ring gate, whereupon he deposits himself in a rather disinterested way against a post; his bulky form, under a well worn cap, and draped in an old brown smock, rests there while his prim, dapper little wife, kitted out in the latest young-thing boots, trousers and top, dashes round the ring after her equally well turned out charge: she, brandishing a curry comb, with which she touches up the bits of the heifer's coat which apparently, to her keen eye, are not quite sufficiently well in place. Whilst this act is stage-managed to perfection, the auctioneer conducts the more serious business of receiving bids from the sober looking buyers, who, after all, came here today to buy good cattle, not be entertained. By the time the hammer drops, the dutiful, disinterested husband has been back again to the pens for another of his wife's very smart entrants for presenting in the ring.

Whether it was, that the third of her pride and joy on this particular day was always a bit temperamental anyway, or maybe, was just fed up with spending the last couple of days shut up in a clean shed, being powder-puffed washed and brushed-up, I couldn't tell: but I suspect the final straw came with the humiliating twitching of that wretched curry comb as she was trotted round that ring. Whatever it was, obviously, for her, enough was enough. Quite suddenly, up went the heifers hind legs, kicking out at the air, and off round the ring she stormed. Realising that her tormentor must be some-where about, she promptly stopped, turned, and seeing the unfortunate beauty therapist, still standing, in a bewildered state, wondering why any progeny of hers should behave quite so badly - she made straight for her in a remarkably threaten-ing way. The auctioneer, aware that the bidding had suddenly ceased, and a deathly hush had settled round the ring, pre-pared to bring his hammer down for the last time; only then did he sense the enormity of that silence, and gazing round at the crowd, noticed the concentrated expressions on their faces. By this time, the bored husband had shaken himself half awake, amazed that a cattle auction could be quite so excit-ing, and prepared himself to watch the events unfold: where-upon, he then became fully awake, and realising that his own wife was one of the star performers, in what was fast becom-ing an equal match to anything the Spaniards could offer as entertainment to their tourists; rushed into the ring, and like a dashing fairy-tale prince, swept his wife to safety through one of the emergency gaps at the ringside. Immediately the victorious little heifer settled back down, and stood quietly in the ring as if waiting for the crowd to burst into applause, but obviously delighted that her bravado had rid her of that fussy little pest.

A new euphoric sense of admiration straightaway took hold of the ringside crowd, and the bidding started up again with a new briskness, vitality and intensity that hadn't been seen at any sale for a long time, for it was plain to see that most of those there must have been thinking that the man who could take this spirited little thing away from the sale that day, would surely be taking home a great prize.

Dolgellau is the heartland for the sale of Welsh cattle. If a man wants to buy a good Welsh bull, that is where he should go. In some sales the bulls outnumber the females, so great is their demand, and men come from as far away as Australia, New Zealand, and Canada to buy them. Some say that at this sale the only people to sell a bull this year, are the ones that bought him last year; and those that buy one now will be back selling him next year: so all they are doing is passing the beasts round amongst themselves when they have finished with them. Well, if that is true, it makes a good time for all of them, for they probably would not see each other from one year's end to the next, if they did not make the excuse to go to the sales. But that is not the way I see it, for each year new young bulls are always to be bought and sold at Dolgellau.

What an Englishman can only do in this part of Wales, is to buy - never can he sell - for a man should always buy upstream from where he lives, and sell downstream. This, when you think about it does make common sense, for never should a man buy an animal born and bred in the softness of the lowlands and expect him to thrive in the harshness of the mountains. That is not to say a beast that is never taken into a shed during winter in some of the high bleak places of England would not be happy in Wales, where many spend their winter in sheds because of the wetness of the climate, and the poaching of the ground; and it is only the poaching of the ground for which they are taken in - never for the sake of the animal. For always they are happier outside than in, with their long thick outer coats to shed the wet; and their fine dry mossy undercoats to keep the warmth against them; and even in the highest of storms will you always find, when the wet is draining from their coats like the water from a gutterless roof, that underneath, amongst the softness of this fine moss, all will be stillness and dry.

A man, not far from where I live in Gloucestershire always kept Welsh cattle, because he was never able to find the money to buy a shed in which to winter his stock, and he said that the Welsh would easily cope with the bad weather. When the time came that he could afford a shed, and he put his beasts in, thinking he was doing them a great favour, they spent all their time walking round the walls, trying to find a way out again. Another bought a handful of Welsh cattle for bringing on to fatten. By the end of the winter they were no bigger than when he put them in his shed the autumn before. "Too hot", he was told by an old friend, "You should've run the clippers along their backs to let the steam come off them, and then they would have grown as well as the others".

Running right down through the west side of Gloucestershire, from the north to the south, is a steep west-facing hillside, where the Cotswold Hills meet the Severn Vale. This Cotswold Scarp, as it is called makes a pretty sight, with its grassy valleys and wooded slopes. Steep, they are, with fine views of the River Severn, twisting its silvery way out towards the Bristol Channel, and then on, losing itself into the great Atlantic.

Looking beyond the river, it is easy on a clear day to see the Welsh Hills, with the Sugar Loaf at Abergavenny in the brightness of the evening sky, standing like a sentinel. The Black Mountains, close to the Welsh Marches, running away to the north, with the dramatic sweep of Hay Bluff completing their finale at the little border town of Hay-on-Wye, nestling at it's foot, and wedged against the river; quiet and undisturbed, as it has lain for centuries.

Perhaps it was the romantic in me which took hold, as I sat on the hill close to home, quietly looking across the evening landscape towards that other country, with its mystic soft blue mountains, and deep silent valleys in the silhouette against the setting sun. For here it was amongst those mountains and valleys I knew men kept sturdy, fine, hardy, black hill cattle. Cattle that would weather anything, and eat anything, and despite all, could still thrive. Cattle that would cope where others would wilt and fail. Or maybe perhaps it was just that my English cross-bred suckler-cows never did well on that rough old hill of ours, which struggled to produce even the poorest stemmy, unpalatable, course and lanky Tor Grass, sharing its space on the limestone brash with a hundred other plants, like Horseshoe Vetch, Wild Orchids, and in the spring, numberless Cowslips.

I was gradually realising, that whether through pure romanticism or, more like, as I would prefer to say, because of common sense practicability, I really must go across that river and on into Wales, and bring back home some of those Welsh beasts for myself, if for no other reason than to learn the difference between my cattle and theirs; but in my deepest mind I was already convinced that they would comfortably cope with this poor place of ours, and that the sooner I went the better.

To bring Welsh cattle into England was not too common, especially where there had been a long tradition of English livestock keeping, and the old favourite Friesian cross Hereford was the long established suckler cow: she being the beast who gives birth to a calf whose father, (sire) would be a beef animal himself; which would then go on to be suckled and reared by the crossbred mother, and would finally, after about one year and a half, or more, be ready for the table. Careful have I been not to sing the praises of these young progeny, for there are not many to be sung.

Since fairly recently, when cranks started ruling our minds and having great input to the British way of life, and who spend time telling everyone that red meat is bad for us, and beef, which has the slightest whiff of fat is even worse, the demand has turned away from what, over the centuries was known as the Beef of Old England, which was produced largely by the good old pure bred Hereford cattle from the lush permanent pastures of our lowland farms; and in the hills of Wales and Scotland, by their own native breeds. But those days have gone, and the cranks rule hard over us, so that now the British beef farmer has to give the public what the so-called experts tell them they must eat, and this is the dry tasteless lean pap of the Continental beasts, such as the Charolais, Limousin, Belgian Blue, and so on. These animals are the sires put to our own English cross bred cows; and what they produce is poor by comparison to the old British native pure breeds. Any connoisseur of meat would say that for the best taste in beef there needs to be the moistness from the delicate traces of fat found in the British breeds. Now fortunately for common sense there is the beginning of a quiet renaissance in the appreciation of eating, and the art of producing traditional beef, all of which I was already aware, and anxious to be a part of. So it was too, I knew these old Welsh cattle would fit that bill exactly.

The final straw, which made me change to the Welsh cattle, came, as I knew it would, in the early summer of that year. My Hereford cross Friesian cows had all calved, down on the lush, south facing permanent pasture next to the house, and the time had come to send them back up on that rough old hill again.

"Shall we give them three days or four, before they are all back at the hill gate bellowing to come down again?" I said to my wife Pat. As it happened, it was on the second day. When I had just finished doing the rounds of the cattle, I was approaching the hill gate to go down. Suddenly I sensed the sound of thundering hoofs behind me, glancing back over my shoulder I saw that the hillside above me was cascading with rushing cows and calves, legs flying, and feet kicking at the air, excited grunts and bellows issuing forth from them in the hopeful anticipation that there might be a chance today that I would let them back to the best grass below again. The disappointment was obviously just too much for them to bear. As I closed the gate behind me, shutting them out, and walked down through the bottom field, stirring up the rich fragrance of the fresh new spring grass as I went; they began to bellow, and they bellowed, each in her turn, most of that day, and the protests continued on and off for a fortnight, until either from hoarseness or weariness, or both, they realised that they must make do with their hill.

It is distracting when going about your work to have discontented animals complaining to you every day, for the hillsides round about echoed with their loud voices, amplifying the sound so that it was like a legion of trumpeting bandsmen, and nowhere could a man escape from it, not even in the depths of his own house. Added to this were the complaints of my wife, who was getting to her usual worked-up state from all the noise.

"Right", I said "that's it, we will start selling all the cows with their calves before they need to go to the bull again. We will go over to Wales and start replacing them straightaway with bulling Welsh heifers, so that we will have them all back here ready to put to a Welsh bull in August, and that will be an end to all this noise": and that is what we did, and that is how it was.

Although, over the years I had made many friends amongst my cows, and I had my favourites which I was very sad to see go; by selling each cow with her calf I knew that they would all be just starting again, new lives on other farms. As long as those calves were kept with their mothers, and there was plenty of food for their bellies, once they were accepted into the new herds by the other cows, after a day or two, or even less, all would be forgotten of their past life, and happiness would settle with them once more. For always it is a great myth that people without knowledge of animal husbandry have, that they think that animals must have the feelings of people; that they have the keen senses of a great memory for the desiring of the past and the worrying for the future. For never is it that stock are overwhelmed with a magical view from a hilltop, or concerned when the haystack or silage clamp begins to lose its size half way through the winter, and the worry of wondering if the food in it will last them until the spring grass begins to grow again. All these things please or worry us - but not so for them. It is always just that they must be well fed, kept healthy, and have others for their com-panions; and that last thing is important, for our farm stock are descended from the beginning of life on this earth, to have lived amongst others, in their flocks and herds, and for a cow or sheep, or horse or pig, or hen to live alone is a sadness for them; and this I say would be to the point of cruelty when they are left endlessly alone in a field or stall, and the worst offenders of this practice are those who would tell you that they are the kindest. Those who have come to be known as the "good lifers", they are the people who are often cruel through their own ignorance and arrogance.

So it was, one by one, with their calves, we said goodbye to our Friesian cross Hereford cows, and at the same time, as we did this, we made sorties into Wales to buy Welsh heifers to replace them.

By now May had arrived, and I took myself off to Dolgellau where there was to be a sale of Welsh cattle. Hopefully I would be able to buy two nice heifers here which I would then bring straight back home to form the beginning of the new herd.

"Have a good journey up?" asked my English-friend-living-in-Wales, as we met in the mart car park. "Perfect as always", I replied. "You know, even if I did that journey every week I think I would never tire of it", I added. Leslie, my English-friend-living-in-Wales, had, with his wife Anna, bought, upon our uncle's retirement, part of his farm some years earlier, and were by now well and truly settled into life in Wales; here they had come; not expecting the "good life" as some of the city slickers, who try to opt out of the rat race for gold, think they will have, when they bring their worldly wealth in a convoy of furniture vans, supported by a healthy bank balance: only to be forced out again a few years later by sheer poverty, returning to England with all they have in the back of a pick-up truck. I am convinced it takes a much shrewder man to scrape a living for his family in Wales, than it does for those parasites who manipulate the money and stock markets in our cities to provide for theirs.

"How has the lambing gone" I asked. Leslie had comparatively little acreage, and he was acutely aware of the hazards of running a small farm, having been reared on one himself, so he was typically philosophical. "Not as well as we hoped - too much rain and cold wind, lost a few lambs from chill", he replied, "perhaps it will be better next year, then we mustn't grumble, maybe the bed and breakfast will be better". Even so, they would manage, just the two of them, never having had that much, they never expected much, everything was paid for, and "if you couldn't pay when you had it, then you shouldn't have it", they always said. Their pleasures came from what they did, and where they lived; and although the price they paid in effort and hard work was high in difficult years, they struggled on. Either a man needs to be born into this sort of life, so that he knows no other, or he must be the sort who puts great store in simple things, and seeks nothing else.

Just the same, bills need paying, and many young sons from hill farms that have been in families for generations are no longer willing to put up with the hardships, and are turning their backs against it all. Where this leaves the future of Wales and the Welsh countryside with its open grazed mountains and emerald pastures I dread to think, for the only alternative to this beauty seems to be the endless, endless tracts of dull uninteresting plantations of conifers, stretching wherever a man cares to look, hoping, hoping for something different, but never finding it. For the farms and families that have moulded the beauty of that landscape over the centuries will have faded away. The hills will never be living places anymore, with their hardy Welsh Mountain flocks of sheep being gathered for dipping, shearing or lambing; depending on the time of year. The Collie dogs; no longer streaking away at the whistle or call of their masters; bringing down the mountainside before them, the white tumbling masses of racing sheep: and the walkers, yes the walkers, who come in their hoards and disgorge by the mini-bus load expecting to tramp, tramp all day long, grinding away the already over worn footpaths under their relentless feet. They come to enjoy these pleasures, and then leave again at the end of the day; never contributing to the local economy with even the purchase of a packet of crisps: but just taking, taking year after year. They too will return no more, for what they had for so long taken for granted was not immortal after all, and none of its beauty will remain here any longer. For too long we have been governed by politicians and civil servants with blinkered vision and urban minds: to them the countryside of our land is unfamiliar, very few of them really understand it, or those who work there. Always, I say, that when every boy or girl leaves school, they should spend twelve months working on the land. Unfortunately, that would not be possible, but if it were, it would save us out here many problems of being advised by those with no understanding, and heads full of half baked ideas and ideals packed in by media half-wits.

It is, too, because of all this, that these sorts seem unaware that this beauty has been worked at for generations in a partnership between man and God. That they are not the new enlightened, bright-eyed pioneering conservationists that they think they are. If only they would stop their babbling and take the trouble to see when they look, and empty their stupid minds of themselves, and be gracious and humble enough to listen to those with the experience, which no amount of book learning can give a man; it will be only then that they will find that all that they are saying about how things should be done, has been the way of things long before their so-called educated minds were even formed. Not long will it be now, if this intelligentsia do not listen to the wisdom of experience; before life and sight of the Welsh mountains and hills, especially, will disappear, and never return again. In the meantime, it is, that most of those who are part of this place often wonder if it will last long enough for even them, with many fearing that for their children, there will perhaps be no hope at all.

Leslie held very strong views about interfering bureaucrats, but at this moment felt he should forget them for once, and enjoy the day. "Shall we go in and have a look at the pens", he said. I agreed, for here you could get close to the stock, and it was the best place to really see what was on offer. "Still not many here yet", I remarked. "They'll all be scrabbling in at the last minute as usual", he replied. We only had fifteen minutes before the sale was to begin, and the pens did look remarkably empty compared with the number of entries in the sale catalogue. This was not good, for it was one thing being able to take your time looking at beasts in the pens, and marking the catalogue with those you were interested in bidding for, and seeing them for the first time from the distance of the ringside, being walked about; and at the same time, getting your head round the slick pace of the auctioneer – You might just happen to end up with something you didn't want, for the price you wouldn't like.

As we browsed the pens in deep discussion of the quality of those heifers which came into the bulling category (approximately two years old), we were suddenly aware of an increase in the activity around us, in fact it was more a frenzied rushing about, than just an increase in activity. Stock were being hustled down the aisles, gates were slamming open and then shut as a batch of four was put into a pen. No sooner had the drover delivered them, than, bearing down upon him again were six more. "Pen twelve," shouted a voice. On they came, and with a skilful twist of his wrist, the drover had the gate of twelve open, and standing with his legs apart, arms extended, in went the new arrivals.

At the far end of the shed, cattle lorries and Land Rovers with a variety of livestock trailers behind them were suddenly arriving in near convoy by now, disgorging their loads: a few with eight or ten beasts, but most with two or four. Out from the backs of the vehicles they came, clattering down the ramps – this lot to the left – that lot to the right. No sooner had all their feet touched the concrete floor of the shed, than the ramp was lifted back again, and the vehicle driven quickly off to make way for the next, which was being smartly reversed into its slot.

As the cattle were settled into their allocated pens, their keepers pottered about making sure their charges looked their best for the ring. In one, a father and son were desperately trying to ear tag a couple of big stroppy calves, a job which I suspect they had wished they had done months ago, when these youngsters would have been more docile, and less strong; but always it is that there is something more pressing to take you away from things, which you know, must in the end be done; and for them it was the end, for no longer would they be able to leave it for another day, because in another day these calves would be somewhere else. Each lot, as it arrived drew a bunch of prospective buyers, carefully eyeing them, some going into the pens and running their hands along their backs, as if hoping to find something of benefit or otherwise which might have been skilfully hidden amongst the long hair. It is often that Welsh cattle will not stand for you like that: for many of them get very little handling, they are quite often farmed from a distance, so to speak, as it is the sheep on most hill farms that take precedence over them, and the cattle fit in round them, and are very seldom too close to a man. I know of one farm, and there will be others, where the cattle can only be looked at from a Land Rover; if you attempt to walk into the field, they are spooked, and are soon gone from you.

As I took a last look about the shed; for the time was near for the sale to begin: over in the opposite aisle, which was reserved for cows with their calves; I noticed, away from the noise and clammer, standing, patiently waiting was a lovely matronly cow with her four week old bull calf beside her. She cudding contentedly - he standing, gazing about in half inter-est - Both seemingly unaware of the noise, hustle and bustle swirling around them. Then, hobbling up the aisle towards them came their owner, and with a quiet murmur, hardly audible, the old man moved the pair forward into the pen reserved for them. As I stood watching the three quietly get-ting settled, it was apparent that a strong bond existed between them, certainly between the man and the cow, a bond which would have grown stronger over the passing years, and would then somehow have been mysteriously passed down to that little calf; and I wondered why it was the three of them were here today. Perhaps, I thought, this old man had grown too old and decrepit to cope any longer, and his family had at last persuaded him to give up what had become so much of himself through all his long life. Never had he probably known anything else. So what now would there be to get him from his bed each morning if he hadn't his few cows to tend: and I wondered then if he had ever thought that the day would arrive when he might be having to sell his old friends off one by one; and if he had ever given a thought to how he would cope with all the facing up to it. Perhaps he had secretly hoped that it would be he who would be carried off first, away from the farm: and I couldn't help wondering for myself; about that too.

Quickly, as these thoughts gripped my mind with sadness, I turned my gaze away from that little group: and as the auc-tioneer emerged, ringing his hand-bell to summon the bidders; we left them, and made our way towards the door, and on through to the ringside.

CHAPTER 4

Sometimes They Surprise Us

The summer of 1992 was the last time we calved our Hereford x Friesian cows. By the following October they had all been sold-on through Gloucester Market, with their calves for breeding.

Of course it was a sad day saying goodbye to old friends, but then we really had no alternative, as they all found it so difficult to cope with the poor grass on our rough old hill. Besides which they were driving us both mad with their continuous loud bellows of protestations.

Whether they knew it was their last summer with us, or maybe, more like, it would have been the weather that year, which caused the increased growth of some of the rarer grasses and herbs on the hill, (fertility drugs – I reckon). Whatever it was, they did us proud, because they went out with a great flurry by producing three sets of twins. Admittedly one of those cows wasn't going, as she was Welsh, although not pedigree. (Bought during the transaction from Hereford x Friesian to Welsh, and before we finally decided to breed pedigree stock).

Anyway, there we were, three bonuses, (although twins do

tend to be small and sometimes troublesome – so they are not always pluses all the time). Nevertheless, we of course were mighty pleased, especially as they all produced without any problems. I say we were mighty pleased; that is not quite true, for the poor unfortunate cow who calved after the three sets were born, was obviously a great disappointment to Pat, because when I gave her the news that another cow had just calved, she responded with: -

"What, - no twins this time? – I couldn't quite understand her attitude on that occasion, because she is normally such a contented person really – Oh well, the worst elements of human nature do sometimes grab hold of even the most decent of us at times, I suppose. Although, I am sure she didn't really mean it in the way it sounded.

The first cow to produce the twins was Nerys, a non-pedigree Welsh animal which we had bought from Dolgellau the previous year.

Normally we only treat our young stock for stomach and lung worms. Being a newcomer to Welsh cattle, and not giving enough thought to the grazing conditions, which exist in Wales. (Very wet, with many cattle drinking from streams rather than water troughs); both being conducive to causing worm infections; I didn't think to worm her for either as she would be considered to be an adult animal. Something, after the following experience, we put right whenever we bought in heifers from Wales.

Needless to say, a short time before Nerys was due to calve she suddenly began to lose weight; and in no time at all her breathing became worryingly rapid. In fact, she looked a perfect candidate for death.

"Send-her-down-the-road-Stephanie" was summoned; (well, it just happened she was available at the time).

Stephanie was one of the young female vets in the practise at the time; a girl with a thick crop of black hair; short and stocky – she knew her stuff – I think – and tended to know everything else as well, but had, at the same time this shocking fetish for wanting to get rid of everything regardless.

"You always want to hang on to your animals, she said to me one day.

"Well, if I listened to you, I wouldn't have any left by now would I?" I replied.

Anyway; here she was; and of course, one look at Nerys brought forth the usual diagnosis, and quick cure – "Send her down the road – she won't last!" she snapped.

"Definitely not – I can't do that – she's going to calve any time now" I retorted.

"She'll never cope with that as well!" came the unsympathetic reply.

It was then I had a flash of inspiration – Whatever I didn't know about Welsh cattle; I did know they were remarkably tough. So, I thought, it's worth a chance.

"Ah – well, that's where you're wrong Stephanie, because you haven't got here a pampered Friesian milker who would have keeled over in that condition long ago by now. What you have here is a tough hardy Welsh hill cow – give her a try – I'll bet she'll survive" I said, with all the authority of a Welsh cattle expert.

Placing her stethoscope to the cow's sides she gave her a thorough examination.

"Bad infestation of lung worms which is causing a serious infection as well – temperature of 105," she said.

"I'll give her an injection for the worms, and put her on a five day course of antibiotics," she added.

Which she did, and with that – she went. No doubt convinced as to who would be proved right.

Five days later, having dropped off a couple of pretty small calves in the meantime; one red, and one black: both looking very smart after being cleaned, polished, and well fed by the patient – Nerys still had this temperature of 105, but was beginning to look a little better.

The next day her temperature dropped to 103; we then decided to put her on a further three-day course of another antibiotic; and within a further couple of days she was well away, and didn't look back again.

She went on to rear the two calves as well as any other cow could have ever reared just one; and at the same time continued to put plenty of condition on herself. - Tough in 'em?

I never could remember if I ever mentioned the result to Stephanie. Wouldn't be prudent really I suppose would it? – Shouldn't like to upset the girl.

"Zoe's been trying to calve for a while now; I think we're going to have to help her." I called to Pat through the kitchen door.

Zoe was always a bit on the small side, and I think if I hadn't been so desperate to get a decent collection of Welsh cattle together to put to the bull by that previous August, I probably wouldn't have bought her. As it was she was here now, so we had to get on with it.

Soon she was in the pen, the calving ropes on, and the pair of us began to pull; one on each front leg of the calf. It wasn't long before things started to happen: the young heifer co-operated perfectly; her contractions working well with our efforts. First a healthy twitching black nose emerged, then, after a bit of a struggle, a head surfaced, with eyes full of life, closely followed by the neck, shoulder and ribs. More gentle pulling – Then some serious pulling: followed by frantic pulling; and no matter how hard we tried, nothing was moving any longer. The calf had become well and truly jammed.

"The hips are caught, Zoe's too narrow to take the calf's hips – We must get the calf away, otherwise it'll suffocate, and we'll lose it" I called to Pat.

Desperately we kept on with our struggle, but it seemed useless, we just didn't have sufficient strength between us.

"If only Richard were here, (Richard is our youngest son, a well-built teenager at the time) his extra strength would get it out" Pat gasped – But Richard was unfortunately out.

It's no good – quick run and call the vet, I'll keep trying", I said.

Within minutes Pat was back – followed closely by Richard – Unbeknown to us, he had been in the house all the time: If only we had realised sooner.

He and I pulled; and the calf was immediately free.

As it slithered to the ground I fell upon it, and shook it, slapping its body to stimulate the breathing; and clearing its nose and mouth of afterbirth – and eventually –

"Too late", I whispered – "It's gone – We're too late – If only." – If only – If only. – How many times during our lives have we ever said, - "If only".

Cwm Parc Eleri 2nd (born June 1992). This would be her first calf.

"Got a breech here," I said, feeling about inside the heifer. "I'd rather be safe than sorry, even if it is eleven o'clock at night, and we'll have to pay the extra for the vet.

Soon Nick the vet arrived, and started to sort things out in the cow: turning the calf until it was the right way round, and then helping it out with the calving aid, "Heifer" I said. –

"I'll just check there isn't another one in there, " he replied, shoving his arm back in again, up to his armpit.

"Well – I've got something" he said – "Calving aid" he called – and soon, out popped a second. "Bull calf this time, pity really; that means the heifer will be a free martin I suppose" I muttered. (A free martin is a heifer, twinned to a bull calf; which means the chances are she won't be able to breed because, whilst the embryo was in the womb, she would have taken on more of the male hormones from the male twin, than she would normally have done if he hadn't been there.) "Better check again in case," he said – Hand plunged in – groped around. "All clear", we can go home now. So after making sure the new arrivals were well settled, we went off to our beds.

By the next morning the heifer calf, who had been the first to be born, was a bit slow at getting started, and needed help to feed. On the other hand, the little bull calf was very busy and sprightly, and got straight on with his feeding. Just the

33

same, because he was the smaller of the two, he got the most attention from his mother. The other; she no doubt thought, being the larger could look after herself, which was completely wrong thinking as it happened. So it befell us to help the heifer calf get to grips with the idea of sucking at a teat, instead of any old bit of hair which happened to come her way, as she groped along her mother's underside. Soon the frustration and coaxing was over and she got the general drift. Being Sunday, we took ourselves off in the afternoon for our usual walk over the hill. As we returned, back down the lane, a near neighbour, whose father used to farm in the next valley, was running up towards us.

"There's something hanging out the back of that cow in the pen", she called.

"Just a bit of afterbirth not come away I expect," I said – "I'll have a look anyway," I added.

As soon as I got into the pen, I thought something was up because Eleri was there, lying down, not relaxing, but busy straining away with contractions. It was then that I noticed, on looking closer – sticking out from her rear – a little black tail –

Yes, she had produced triplets – although, of course, the third one was well and truly dead by now.

But where had she been all this time – It was obvious Nick had done a thorough job in feeling around inside the cow for anyone else, because I had watched him myself; but the poor little mite must have been so far down in the womb that she was completely out of reach –

The chances of triplets? – Apparently 3000 to one in cows.

"That's a blooming rig you've got there" said the owner of a bunch of young Friesian Holstein heifers, which my Charolais cross (steer?) was busy chasing about his field, after demolitioning an admittedly shaky 40 ft length of fence to get at them.

It so happened a few weeks earlier, a maiden lady who kept horses, which weren't keeping up with the eating of all the grass she had about the place, had asked if I would be interested in renting some of it from her.

Knowing that my beasts were generally quiet, and her fences were quietly falling down, I nevertheless thought it wouldn't be a problem; so I agreed.

Now, before going on, I will explain what a rig is.

On stock farms: as in real life: 50% of births are female; which leaves 50% of the other sort.

In real life, 50% of each sort is a happy balance, except, I suppose, when people start mucking about with things, and end up grabbing lots of extra females, like some of the more wealthy do out there in the desert. Although they had the same problem in Old Testament times, but must have largely got over it by turning some of the surplus males into eunuchs.

On stock farms – what we want, if it's dairy, are plenty of females to turn into cows. But you can't because its 50/50 – So you're stuck with it.

On beef farms – with suckler cows – which we are – 50/50 will do fine. Some females can stay in the herd for breeding, and the rest of the females can be sold for someone else to do some breeding.

But you still have the other 50%, which are males; so eventually they get onto everyone's dinner table for eating.

Just the same, if you want a quiet life while these eating beasts are growing up, it's no good just hoping that these males will give you it if you don't do something about them to start with: (although you are allowed to do nothing to one or two, because if you fix them all, you'll stop getting calves, and then that will be the end of your business). NB. Don't use your own unfixed males on your own females, because all sorts of odd things might happen. Always use someone else's, but not close relatives; (beasts not people that is – Although close relatives – people could be a problem too, if the beast turns out to be).

Anyway, those who are not the privileged few have to be fixed; and there are several ways of doing this, although, just for the time being we will only be referring here to one of them. – That is the rubber band method.

In a nutshell, (and don't try this with any old rubber band). What you do is stick a rubber band, on what might be described as the offending parts of the beast, when it's still a calf; and you will find that eventually they will fall off – No pain, no suffering – but what a difference.

As a young man; when I worked on dairy farms, it was easy. A few days after any male calves were born, you went into the calf pens with a mate, and between you, you caught this lively little calf, because he could only run round and round the pen. So eventually, because he couldn't get out, you were able to bring him down with a rugby tackle; and while one of you sat on him to keep him still, the other chap whacked the rubber band on him with the special pliers supplied for the job. – Simple – after a few weeks; if you had done the job properly, the little fellow had become sexless – and wouldn't have a clue about it, and wouldn't care less either.

Now, with suckler cows whose calves are born outside, (healthier and cleaner). If you leave the rubber band operation for too long, (like say, the next day after the calf is born) the chances of catching him in a field rather than the confines of a calf pen, are pretty remote. So to get over the problem you have to make sure the job is done whilst he is still recovering from being born, and in a happy sleepy state; which means – as soon as possible. The disadvantage with doing it this quickly is that his testicles may not have always "descended". This could then mean, that when you pop the rubber ring on, you may not catch everything you were hoping to catch. Consequently, the rubber ring then prevents the offending object from descending when it is ready and is attempting to do so. So, having sat up there inside the beast until the rubber ring eventually falls off, it obligingly stays where it is, out of harms way, but still connected to the happy organs. Thus causing him to have all the impulses and desires of an entire male (bull), but none of the fertility to do the job. – Hence, he is called a Rig – (but don't ask me why). Unless it could be one of the definitions from the Concise English Dictionary – "To indulge in practical joking". Which I suppose is what our rig would appear to be up to – With intentions – but not serious about it.

Anyway, here we were with this rig, causing mayhem to everything and everyone he came into contact with: and if we weren't to fall out with the neighbours we would need to do something pretty smartish. So we did – and he was whisked off home in double quick time, penned up out of harms way, and the vet summoned to perform the necessary alterations.

"Right" said Michael Staley (vet), choosing a new blade for his veterinary Stanley Knife.

"Whatever you do, once I have given him the injection, you must immediately open the gate of the crush, so that he can walk out before the injection takes effect and he falls to the ground. Because if he collapses in here, in the crush, I will never be able to work on him; there just isn't enough room".

Having got myself into a good position to operate the crush gate in the blinking of an eye: Staley selected a good vein on the beast; slowly pushed in the needle; said "Ready?" Squeezed the syringe, and "Hey Presto" – the rig dropped straight to the ground. – before I could even flex a muscle to spring my arm into action to open the gate.

"Well, I'll be dammed," exclaimed Staley, looking down in bewilderment at the crumpled motionless form lying before us.

"It's still alive I hope?" I moaned

"Well – yes, thank goodness" he returned.

"So what now?" I asked, wondering just how he was going to set to work on this 6-cwt mass of twisted creature.

"Nothing for it, but to get it out," he retorted.

"How?" I said.

Now Michael Staley was no mean sized bloke – over 6 ft and well built with it. But, at the same time, not the sort you see pulling double-decker buses about with their teeth.

"Open the gate" was all he said in reply to my last question. Obediently I obliged, while he placed himself over the sleeping animal – Legs apart, he reached down, grabbed hold of its tail, and pulled it upwards, heaving with all his strength, until the hindquarters began to lift from the ground. – Continuing to pull, he then began to lift in a forward direction, so that the rear of the animal started to roll over that which was still lying on the ground (a somersault, in fact). Slowly he continued this movement, using all his strength, and as he did, the beast began to roll through the gate onto the open space outside.

Where, upon landing, he promptly got up, and walked away!

Having been made look stupid twice by this fake bull, we were both determined by now, that we weren't going to be tricked a third time. So, with renewed enthusiasm, we quickly rounded up the half doped beast, gave him another shot of sedative; let him out of the crush at double-quick time; where he gently keeled over allowing Staley, with knife brandishing, to jump on him, and deal the fatal blow to his pseudo masculinity.

Needless to say, after that, we ditched the rubber rings, and have resorted to bloodless castrations – and if you want to know all about them – ask your vet.

CHAPTER 5

I'm Sure it Wasn't Meant To Be Like This

Calving time is always fraught, ever-new experiences lurk round every tree and new day. Never do I approach May with a light heart and a happy attitude towards the hurdles of the next few weeks. You would think that bringing a new life into the world would be a joyful occasion, and so it is, but it is the preliminaries running up to that moment which cause the strife and stress.

"Oh no! I don't believe it – What's that hanging out of the back of Gwen" I muttered to myself. I had just come down off the hill from my morning walk round the cattle, and into the bottom field, where we kept the waiting-to-calve-cows. Here was a good place to watch events, it was close to the house, and a quick walk round at any time of day, (or night) would generally give me a good idea of the progress or the problems – and here was a problem.

I was just about to leave for a nice leisurely trip, and a

couple of relaxing days at Dolgellau, for the Ancient Cattle of Wales committee meeting. This was the cattle society which had been formed to include the Welsh cattle of all colours other than black; those colours which I have already mentioned at the beginning of this book.

"So what is going on; we still have more than two weeks before the arrival of the first calf? Just what I needed, Sod's Law rules supreme again", I thought. "Well, that's the end of my outing".

As I got over to her, I could see that we had a vagina prolapse. "This will be her 4th calf, we've never had trouble before – I suppose she's been sleeping on a steep bank and the weight of the calf inside her has shoved everything out", I mumbled. "Oh well, I'm going to shove it all back in again; tell Pat to keep an eye on her tomorrow morning, and if there is a problem, I shall be back by early afternoon, and I can sort it out then; and hope, that for now I will be able to go away and forget it – Should be alright though – Pat likes practising her midwifery anyway, even if she last did it on a human thirty years ago. – Good to keep abreast of things. – So that's what I did; and that's where I went; and that's how we managed.

"How's Gwen?" I asked Pat as I walked in through the door after my trip. "OK – didn't come out again." I wasn't sure whether I detected just a slight hint of disappointment in her voice as she spoke those few words. I bet she would have enjoyed having a go at that. Given her a sense of achievement, with a bit of nostalgia thrown in, I reckon. Anyway, I was glad she didn't need to. "Good, let's hope it stays there", I said – but it didn't. The next day Gwen saw me coming; and shot the lot out again.

After the third day of this ping ponging, I decided to move her and her sister, for company, to some level ground. "Hopefully that should do the trick," I said. – But it didn't. "Beginning to turn into a nasty habit. Better ring the vet, perhaps he's got some bright ideas," I said.

"Yes", was his verdict over the phone. "That's a vagina prolapse; common in pregnant ewes." "What about cows?" I asked. "Rare; very few cases," he came back. "Typical" I retorted; "if there is anything rare going, we'll get it. When you think of all those chaps with two or three hundred milkers, and me with my handful of suckler cows – I am the mug to get a "rare". Well what can you do about it?" "Stitch her up" he replied. "But mind, she won't calve through the stitches; you'll need to be there when she calves to cut them, otherwise there will be trouble". Just what I needed, we hadn't a clue when she was about to calve, only that it would be during the next month, judging by the look of her. If you run a bull with your cows up on a hill, it's anyone's guess when he serves them. You might be lucky and spot the odd one or two bulling when you just happen to be there; but most of the time these liaisons seem to be conducted on the strictest clandestine terms. Or someone is always on the look out to give them the tip off when you approach.

"So what shall I do, carry on shoving it in, and hope she will calve within the next day or two, or stitch her up and hope for the best," I thought. I opted for the first; I would give her a couple more days. "Right" came the Jordie vet's voice at the other end. "Give us a ring if you want her stitched up; but it's very important to be there when she calves. I remember, when I was out in Australia, had to stitch one of those up – Told them – Keep her in front of the kitchen window so you can watch her. There were eight of them gawking at me doing the sewing up, so one of them must have heard what I said. Four weeks later; got a phone call to say she was found out in the bush, dead, trying to calve through the stitches – threatened to sue the practice."

I've never stayed up day and night for a month, and I don't ever remember meeting anyone who has stayed up day and night for a month either. So if we're lucky she'll calve before I might have to do that – but she didn't. So two days later, with a phone call to the vet. – "Better send someone over to sew this cow up after all." I said.

Now whether it is that all New Zealand vets are pessimists or whether it was just that Nick was. I am not sure. A friend said she thought it was something to do with the farms out there having so many sheep and cattle that it made them very casual; and that, if they had a problem they just threw it away, or you got rid of it somehow. Well, back here, especially if you are in a small way, and struggling – and who isn't; you just can't afford to think like that: every beast has to count, and count very dearly too,

"Well there we are," said Nick, after he had sorted her out with his sewing. "tough old hides on these Welsh cattle, aren't they?

"Good wasn't she – didn't bat an eyelid even though I reckon there was no point on your needle," I replied, proud of owning such a well-behaved beast.

Nick was just about to change my jokey state. "So when she calves I have to cut the stitches, and will she prolapse again then?" I asked. "Yep", came the short reply. "And will it be a full uterus prolapse this time?" I asked. "Yep" he said. "And next year, will she have a vagina prolapse again". I whimpered, dreading the reply. "Yep". He clipped. "So really I should get rid of her then?" "Yep". He said in apparent triumph.

By now I was wondering if this chap hadn't got a heart, or had been sent over by the New Zealand government to undermine our confidence, and get us all to pack it in, so they could have the British meat market to themselves. Anyway, which ever it was, he had done a pretty good job on me that day. Not only was I going to have to stay up night and day for perhaps a month to watch this cow. When she did eventually calve, I was going to end up with the whole lot in my lap, and then try to untangle the calf from the inside of the cow, and hope to come out with a live calf and a live cow. – What a hope. Someone was not going to make it, either me, the calf, the cow, or maybe the whole lot of us.

The next few days were fraught, thinking about it. I decided that if anyone was still going to be here at the end, it would be me, so I wouldn't be staying up all night after all. I reckoned if I saw her last thing at night, and she looked settled, and again first thing in the morning, and regularly during the day, hopefully that would do. This should leave only a short time when things might happen, hopefully, not long enough to cause a problem.

After the third night, I arrived the following morning in the field as usual. Something was hanging from her. Had she tried to calve, and was this a bit of shredded calf that had squeezed through between the stitches? If so what were its chances? How long had it been like this? There were no signs of anything happening late that night. "Typical, typical, Sods law again. The odds were loaded against you anyway," I thought. "Why do I still carry on with all this nonsense – just for peanuts too?"

"She seems quite calm and normal," I thought, as I got nearer – "Can't be too bad, otherwise she would be fretting about." I muttered to myself. "she doesn't look as if she has been struggling at all."

"No – that's not a calf, it's the afterbirth, the waters have burst; the timing couldn't be better, she's just about to get down to the serious business of calving. Now, the next job is to get her into the pen where we can hold her under control. So we did, I cut the stitches, and within less that half an hour she had produced a nice little bull calf without any problems at all, and no sign of Sod either – we had a perfect calving. Well, Nick got that bit wrong; no sign of any sort of prolapse whatsoever.

Even so, despite my misgivings about him having a secret agenda to destroy the British livestock industry by lowering everyone's morale. He was, as it happened, dead right about Gwen's future. We would get the same problems with her every time she approached calving time; this was the agreed consensus of opinion, which I had been seeking over the following few months. So that left us with no choice; poor Gwen would have to go, even though she was still a relatively young cow; and all you can say on these occasions is that it is, "Just one of those things," and grin and bear it; or to use another agricultural phrase, "Where you have livestock, you have deadstock" – Hard world, isn't it!

Talking about prolapses reminds me of another we had shortly after changing to Welsh cattle. Fortunately for us it was a beautiful warm May day, and fortunately for us, someone had spotted the problem, and called in to let us know. We weren't expecting anyone to calve just yet, so the cows were still all on the hill, including the problem we had just learned about.

Off we went, and sure enough, we soon came across Eleri standing there with a very healthy looking bull calf lying next to her, although not cleaned up or fed yet. Eleri herself, from the front looked fine, eyes alert, and more than ready to show off this lovely calf which she thought she had made such a brilliant job of bringing into the world.

It's not what people tell you, it's what they don't tell you that's important, I think, sooner or later through life, is a lesson we all learn. Animals, actually aren't much different, because of course immediately she turned her back towards us; there it was; what looked like pretty well everything that was inside her, turned outside; hanging there in a great dangling mass, and which every time she turned and shifted about swung precariously to and fro, from side to side like an enormous pendulum, just waiting to break away from her; which would then immediately strike her down stone dead.

It wasn't long before the vet arrived, but the problem then was, because we were unable to confine her there on the hill, every time he attempted to start to stuff everything back inside again, she side stepped him, sloshing the stuff all about her, "There's nothing for it", he said at last. "We'll have to gently walk her down to the pen where we can tie her up". – Walk her down to the pen was about 1/8th of a mile, half of it downhill. – Uphill is where cows walk slowly – Downhill is where they tend to run, unless they are half dead, and if she was tempted to run, because she didn't feel half dead, she would be a goner straightaway, with all the force of the violently swinging womb, and then it would be bound to break away, and sever a main artery.

The twenty minutes that followed were pretty tense, something like walking with a suicide bomber, all kitted out with explosives strapped around him, which if he happened to trip, would blow him to bits. The only difference between that scenario and us with her, was that if she didn't watch out, it would be only her who would be the one to go.

When we eventually arrived at the pen, the three of us began to relax, and with a bucket of clean warm water, her womb was gently doused down, and the stuffing-in started. Pounds and pounds of the slippery mass, sliding and slithering about amongst the vets fumbling fingers. Once it was a little over half way in, things became easier, as the weight of what was inside began to drag that which was still left outside; - in; and eventually, with a final slurp, the last vestige disappeared out of sight.

With his arm following closely behind the offending material, and soon up to his armpit inside the patient, the vet set about putting everything in its rightful place. Once he had achieved this, the final polish had to be brought about, and an old lemonade bottle served for this purpose, getting the desired effect by extending his arm by about another 15 inches, so that he could reach the furthest most parts of the cavernous space within the patiently waiting cow.

Having assured himself that all was how it should be, the job was completed with a smart piece of needlework on her vagina, to prevent the lot sloshing back out again.

On reflection, we did have a remarkably easy task bringing that cow down off the hill, considering she had just left her newborn calf behind. The next urgent job was to get back up there and bring the poor little soul down to his mother. As it happened, the place where he was lying was just a neighbour's field – distant, away from the road, which meant we could get the car fairly close to him. The fact that it was a hot day, and he was lying in the sun's warmth must have saved his life, as he hadn't been stimulated by his mother's licking, and by the time we got to him, he was still contentedly sleeping. Quickly we bundled him into the car, and by the time we arrived back at the pen, Eleri was starting to look about for him, now that her mind had been taken off the heavy weight that had been swinging about her rear, and she was beginning to feel normal again.

So the job of reuniting them was a simple matter, as both by now were more than ready for the other, and she immediately obliged by standing; and he by sucking.

The next episode is a series of days I have lifted straight out from my diary. The two heifers referred to here (Florence and Jade) were half sisters from the same farm, they were two of my first pedigree acquisitions.

After our Hereford Friesian cross cows, I initially bought non pedigree Welsh cattle, and it was then, only a matter of time before we decided to start buying pedigree stock, and thereby hope to earn ourselves more money by selling all the female progeny from these for breeding. Being rather naïve about pedigree cattle, I made the fatal mistake of thinking that everything that appeared in the ring must be good. I was about to learn a hard lesson.

To be fair; as 18 month old heifers, these two; Florence and Jade, to me anyway looked pretty good, but even so, sometimes as an animal grows older all the bad shapes and bumps seem to emerge from nowhere, and you begin to wonder why you had bought the thing in the first place. Convinced that you bought what you saw, the only answer must be that they couldn't have possibly looked like this on the day you bought them.

What is it they say? If you want to know how your girlfriend is going to turn out when she's older – Take a look at her mother. Of course, in a cattle sale ring you don't often have that advantage. There is a lot to be said then, for paying a little extra and buying animals which are older, by which time you have generally got some indication of their eventual conformation; and hopefully, don't get any nasty surprises later on. As it happened, we were landed with these two, and suffered badly as a result, right from their first calving when they both produced dead calves. The diary of events which follow, were from the start of their second calvings one year later:-

Sunday 29th May Florence eventually calved (heifer calf) at about 2pm. Calf unable to get up; subsequently unable to feed. Left calf in the hope it would get going.

Monday 30th May (early) No such luck, this calf is still down. Brought it into livestock trailer near pen. Florence tied in pen, to milk out colostrum. What a bashing we took (remember these cattle are not used to being milked). Eventually managed to get enough colostrum from her before we decided to let the bitch go. The colostrum we fed to the calf from a bottle and teat.

Monday 30th May (5pm) Jade showing signs of calving. By the time we went to bed at 11.30pm two feet had emerged. Because of last year's dead calves from these two, we have been giving them selenium and copper over the last twelve months, which hopefully will improve things.

Tuesday 31st May Came out to look at Jade at 1.30 am. Still no progress, although the calf is properly presented inside her. Bearing in mind the problems we had with F+J last year, thought it prudent to get vet straightaway rather than attempt anything ourselves, and then get into trouble. Jade is now at the bottom corner of the field. Michael Staley (vet) arrived at 2am. After a long struggle we managed to get a big bull calf off her using the calving tackle. Jade didn't want to know it, and neither did she by next morning.

Brought calf up near pen, managed to milk Jade very quietly – fed to calf with bottle and teat. This calf has very badly folded back front legs, so he can't get up either. (This condition is not uncommon, and calves will generally eventually learn to walk, and the more they do, the straighter their legs become, until they are normal).

Florence. Put calf outside in sun, so it is now beginning to stand up. This is a funny looking creature, with pop eyes, front leg protruding out in front; and very small. In fact. I suppose – a runt. Nevertheless, by late afternoon she got going, fed herself and went off with her mum. Very rewarding happy sight, although I am not going to register this poor little specimen with the breed society. Can't see her ever making anything of herself.

WED 1ST JUNE - Jade's calf is now in trailer being bottle-fed, he is a lousy sucker, so we are having to resort to feeding him with a tube into his stomach.

THURS 2ND JUNE - Jade. Now before we can even think of getting mother and son together, he has to get on his feet – by now he can stand on his back feet, his front feet are still folded under, although occasionally he is managing to get his right foot in place.

FRI 3RD JUNE – Jade's calf walking much improved. Gone onto milk powder, as still unable to suck, although a very strong calf. We are both beginning to get pretty fed up with this feeding, as it is so time consuming.

Florence. All is well here, and she is determined to care for this funny little creature.

Gwenan (third problem) 5pm She is starting to get restless. By 11pm we decided to go to bed – nothing happening.

SAT 4TH JUNE Gwenan (early) Sure enough, on this drizzling damp day she has produced the tiniest little heifer calf I have ever seen, so small I was able to tuck it under my arm and carry it into the copse, and put it under some straw to get her warmed up. – Because. Guess what? Yes, she can't walk either – I don't believe it – What are we doing wrong. Now, is it us, or the breed? Not content with this, Gwenan is very protective and consequently dangerous. Quite different from the way she normally is.

Sun 5th June Gwenan's calf feeding colostrum through tube into stomach, as she is a poor feeder. By end of day we are still struggling with the slow feeding. Calf getting listless breathing poor. Decided to put her on a course of antibiotics

Mon 6th June Gwenan's calf slightly better, although she takes 1/2 hour to suck 1/2 pt. Need to get at least 4 pints per day into her – What a chore.

Tues 7th June Eleri (4th problem) Looked at her at about 3pm – just the front legs protruding. Went back at 5pm. Couldn't believe it. Enormous dead heifer calf lying on ground beside her. This is her 4th calf, never had problems before.

Thurs 9th June I have suggested that we give up on Gwenan's calf – still taking 1/2 hr to take 1/2 pt. Pat wants to persevere. We have decided to give her two more days. If no improvement will get vet to put her down, as there could be other problems, especially being so small.

Fri 10th June Tim vet came to take blood samples to see if we can learn why we are suddenly having all those problems (possible B.V.D. Bovine viral diarrhoea) which cause small weak calves. Also took pituitary gland from Eleri's calf to check for iodine deficiency.

Sat 11th June Gwenan's calf – all of a sudden is able to suck from the bottle (Talk about an eleventh hour job). The next task is to get her on her mother.

MON 13TH JUNE Jade's calf is a fighter. She is a lousy mother, he really has to hang on to her to get his feed; she keeps walking away. He tends to creep up on her, and goes between her back legs whilst she is grazing so that she doesn't know what's going on. He is what I call a "back ender". You can always tell "back enders", they wear skullcaps; that is dung pats which drop on their heads from their mothers as they feed.

TUES 14TH JUNE Jade's calf is obviously getting plenty of grub from somewhere else as well; he looks extremely well fed.

FRI 17TH JUNE Have discovered Jade's calf is getting topped up from Gwenan so this means he is now being fed by two cows. In the meantime we are still trying to get Gwenan's calf onto her.

We have given Gwenan's calf one more try, when Heledd calved (a cow with always plenty of milk – enough for two calves). Although the cow stood for him to suck he is so petrified of cows, (don't ask me why), it was impossible, and we had to give up.

We never did succeed in getting Gwenan's calf onto a cow. She was always bucket fed by us. Stupid, when you have all those lactating cows about, to have to do the job yourself.
The results from the blood and pituitary gland came back negative, which was a good thing. Decided to give Florence and Jade one more chance to produce good calves next year.

By the middle of May the following year Florence came on bulling, which meant that sometime during that previous winter she had slipped (aborted) a calf. So we decided that enough was enough, and she would have to go. I think we had given her more than a fair chance. After all, out of a possible three calvings, she had only produced one calf, and that was a runt.

Jade, on the other hand, wasn't a lot better. We had another difficult calving (heifer calf). As soon as the calf was out lying on the ground her mother went straight over to the gate to be let out of the pen. I suppose in human terms, we might have called her a career girl. – Once you had produced the goods, in came the "wet nurse", and au pair, and out you went to get on with your life. But even if these corporate dolly birds can get away with it, Jade wasn't going to, and after the usual hard slog for a couple of days, we eventually convinced her where her real responsibilities as a mother lay.

By now we were really sure of what we had had our suspicions of for sometime; and that was that Florence and Jade must have been the result of some serious in-breeding; and unfortunately for us, we had borne the brunt of it. Nevertheless this was the one and only time it ever happened to us. As for the breeder, thank goodness, I no longer see his name in the breed society's herd book, so hopefully no other unsuspecting individual has been caught out.

CHAPTER 6

The Life She Never Knew

April was like June that year, beautiful warm sunshine, everything that should have blossomed into life did; even the May in the hedgerows came that month. The grass in the field near the house was even better than usual, and produced masses of thick lush emerald green meadow fescue and cocksfoot, making the cattle seem to have shorter legs than they already had. The dense blackness of their coats stood in stark contrast against the vivid backdrop of the green slopes.

March had been a wet month, and left the soil black with moisture, and although the stock had spent their winter on it, the sudden warmth of that spring sunshine brought its reward and its rich harvest. Everywhere about them sprang forth with the splendour of natures best. For it is the spring of each year, as it is in the spring of our lives that the pure goodness of God's creation will be seen. The delicate greens of the fresh leaves of the beech woods gathered along the scarps and valleys, which shelter the vale from the east, where they have stood for hundreds of years, drawing the scant moisture from the limestone brash of the edge of the wold. A thousand shades of green, which change through even more, as the sunlight comes and goes between the branches, and every tree that stood, even the oak, by now had burst its hardness to send their green shoots forth. That is, every tree except the ash, she seems not to share the joy of spring as the others do; close to her she clutches the greenness of her tiny leaves within, folded in their tight, lifeless buds. Would we ever see her come to life? Perhaps that reluctance is born from knowing of the shortness of that life, for the warmth of spring and summer seem soon gone; and autumn, from round the corner of another day, will suddenly appear, on a sharp early frost, which will loose those leaves, still green from summer, away from their branch, and they will be gone for ever, swept away on a cold east wind. Even so, and despite this, she always, in the end has to give up what is within her, and bring it forth; bursting, to enjoy the happiness of summer. As late as mid June I have seen an ash tree take, to begin to leaf.

There sometimes is of course, when winter, or time, or maybe endless other reasons prevent a tree from giving out this life again in spring; and she will stand there, in her place, full of sadness within the bareness of her branches, gaunt and naked for all to see, and we feel an urgent need to remove her bleaching dead frame; with the bark blown from its place, and cast in shrivelled scallops about the ground on which, for long years, her leafy shade has spread. No longer will the cattle use that shade, or shelter from the wind and rain, for time has changed that place, and will, still more, as time goes on. For it is, the sights we see that are caused by things which are always about us changing. So it is, when we save a sapling in a hedge, to grow to a mighty tree, for others to enjoy long after we have left this place.

For this is the way of things we know; that life shows forth her beauty, and death stalks with his sadness. But what of life that never was, that came as hope and promise. The mark, which on the calendar, draws nearer the time which would end the nine whole months of waiting.

I wonder when it is, that the big gentle black coated cow becomes aware that the one she is still suckling will soon have to provide for himself, because another, still invisible from their sight, is waiting silently for the time when he will instead, have her care. Is it that she feels the extra weight as she grazes the sloping hillsides; or perhaps it is the bulge she notices, as we might, in our own sorts? I think it isn't any of this, but she will know, for the instinct of animals is a stronger power than we can ever experience, or even begin to understand. Many times I have wondered about this instinct - the understanding that these beasts have of what we think, with our superior minds, is hidden from them, and I am sure the instincts of motherhood must be amongst the strongest which will over-whelm a cow, and she will look prime and fit and healthy. As we call in our own "blooming".

Waen-Oer Awen 7th looked like this. We had bought her five years earlier as a handsome 2 year old bulling heifer from a remote, wild windy place on the south side of Cader; a bleak cold wide valley, where the few trees which survive look as though they spend their time reaching after the last wind to pass by, and that their only desire is to be loosed of that wretched place, so that they might be free for ever from its fierceness. Even though it was a June day and the sun shone down across the bare rugged landscape, it provided little com-fort; for the outcrops of hard rocks dominated everything. Alongside the road, the grass on the flat land in the valley floor competed with great clumps of rushes thriving in the marshy, peaty soil. Every so often the boundary fence at the roadside would be broken by a gate, and a long rough track leading off, twisting and turning its way amongst rock and bog to a huddle of farm buildings, many of which had long been abandoned by those who had finally succumbed, and given up the struggle against the weather, and the harsh real-ities of the market place. The land and stock would then have been bought by a neighbour hoping, that by increasing his acres, flocks and herds it might enable him to keep pace with his falling income, and which might allow him to hang onto the farm which had been in his family for so long. Unfortunately, to do this he would likely need to borrow, and perhaps, heavily. If the price for lambs remained good until he was clear of debt, all would be well, that is, if his health held out too, and he was able to cope with the longer hours he had burdened himself with. For extra work would not mean extra help and every penny would be needed to keep the bank from the door. How else can a man face himself again if he fails to keep the inheritance, handed to him by long generations of hard working ancestors. He must do everything in his power not to be the one to have that snatched from him, and it is this proudness that often shackles him to a life of toil and worry.

"So you got here then - nice to meet you both". Gareth Rowlands came across the rough stone yard, hand held out, and a broad grin on his dark pleasant face. He would be a man in his thirties, slight but wiry, typically Welsh in appearance, and probably from a long line of farming stock, which had existed on this place where we were standing for hundreds of years. I shook his hand eagerly, there was, I felt an instant bond between us, which showed in the response from Pat too, as he shook her hand. These Welsh, I thought, always do welcome you so well, a genuine welcome, not for thinking what they can get from you. Pleased, they are to see that you like their stock so much as to want to buy them. Pleased they are to share in the enthusiasm of keeping and caring for animals, and having the challenge of breeding fine beasts,

"I've got several here for you to chose from", he said, as he led us through between the old buildings to a steep little stone cobbled yard surrounded by a high wall. "Now then, what do you think of them"? He spoke quietly, but with the confidence of someone who knew that what he had before us was good, and they were good too. Gently he stood back to allow us chance to admire the eight fine heifers. They were all of the same age, and ready to put to the bull, good strong, deep and long in the body, big friendly heads, short heavy legs, broad straight backs, and wide hind quarters: their coats were still long from the winter, but soft and sleek just the same; everything about them was as it should be for the breed. As we walked amongst them, they remained as calm and placid as if they had known us all their lives. "Nice temperament too, and I can't remember seeing such an even bunch of grand cattle for a long time", I said. How was I going to choose two out of this lot, I thought to myself. "Not a lot between them, is there"? I remarked. "Well no, they're all good, don't you think?" Said Rowlands, in the matter-of-fact way the Welsh always had, and you knew he meant it, this man knew his cattle. His father before him had always taken a great pride in his black cattle, and although he still helped at the farm, he was quite happy to let the younger man get on with it. "Well, I think they are all too close, it must be a question of which ones are out of the best lines, then mustn't it?" I said, knowing that he would tell me the truth, for here was a man who could be trusted, and would take a pride in having a contented buyer.

Soon our Welshman was giving a potted family history of each of the beasts standing here before us. "She should make an easy calver, never had a problem with any of those": and "They grow well", or "Placid bunch them", and so on. Gradually I began to select the characteristics I thought were important to me in a cow, and soon I had picked out the two that seemed to come closest to that, we drew them out from the rest and penned them up separately. "If I had the money I would like to take them all", I said, glancing at the livestock trailer on the back of our car: easy to say that my boy, I thought. Where do you think you would put them all to get them back home even if you did have the money. Imagine trying to cram eight beasts into a two beast trailer, and for a moment I watched in my mind's eye the three of us pushing and scrabbling as we tried to force them in, the sides of the trailer bulging, and the loud protests sounding forth from the animals.

"Come and have a cup of tea, and I'll sort out the certifi-
cates". I jumped to, with the sound of Rowlands voice. Fully
awake now, we both followed him into the house, where his
wife and two young children were waiting.

All too often, people who have been on holiday in Wales for
the first time, come back complaining bitterly about the way,
they say the Welsh have shunned them. We have great difficulty understanding this, and can only assume that it is that they
expect the Welsh to be always speaking English, and that if
they are not, it must be because they do not want the English
to understand what they are saying, not giving it a thought
that these people are using their native tongue. For I know,
that once they know you are English, then they switch immediately if it is to you they are speaking, and their hospitality is
the same too.

Now when the Welsh sell you cattle from their farms, and
everyone is feeling happy in themselves for knowing that the
other party is happy too, then we all sit down round their
table and enjoy each others company, and all the cooking that
ever comes out of an oven. Then those are the times that
always remain with you, when you think that what you are
doing is not just breeding and caring for lovely beasts: but you
are finding people tucked away in secret corners of the land;
people who want to share themselves with you. People, who,
most of their lives, speak another language and sometimes go
for days without seeing another soul; and yet, when you walk
into their homes, and their lives, it is as if they have always
known you, and that the language they speak is no different
from yours, for they switch from theirs to yours as naturally as
if they hadn't. It is times like this that make you feel humble,
for here are ordinary, honest, hard working folk; and even
their children will talk with you as plainly as anyone, in words
that are so familiar to you but to them are rather strange: and
yet, when, you are gone, never a word of English might pass
between them again for weeks.

The price all decided, with the instructions of how to get

there over the telephone the week before. It was I who had to make the mention of money, and it was the feeling that it was a pity to spoil the atmosphere that was around us, with such coarse things as money, for it should be that all this was being done just because we enjoyed it. "£600 each - a cheque will be fine." That too had been decided last week - and who was to say that we two, who that little Rowlands family had never set eyes on before, and who lived where we said we did, 150 miles away, were not a couple of crooked, slick English cattle dealers, and that when we drove off and a week later the cheque came back, "refer to drawer - no funds", whatever would they do? The two years and nine months, a lot of work and risk which the Rowlands had had, would be gone for nothing. But the Welshman had agreed that he should sell to us, and that I should pay for two, 2 year old Welsh heifers; and that is what they all expected to happen, and that is exactly what did happen. Why should anyone think differently?

Life is still based on utmost trust amongst some, but they are a depleting number I fear, and what a great pity this is for us all.

An hour or so later, the two heifers were loaded, quiet like lambs. Never in their minds did they wonder why they were doing this, or where they would be going, never did they feel the strangeness of walking into this little stall on wheels, where they had never walked before; and where they would be taken far away from their home, from those familiar sur-roundings, and the ones they had been reared alongside, and spent their short lives so far with. No more would they look up from their grazing at the majestic Cader above them, or the distant Snowdon beyond them; and no more would they return again to this place; this place, where they had known no other.

As we drove down the rough track, over the stream and through the boundary gate, with our innocent, trusting new charges trailing behind us, contently cudding in their little stall, there was the feeling of happiness in that car at having had the pleasure of spending the last couple of hours with such delightful people; some new friends, and the hope that we might one day go back again. As for the two in the trailer - they looked happy enough for they were with each other, and were both to settle down to their new life in Gloucestershire. If nothing else,' the trees never stay bent when the wind has gone, down there.

We were now expecting Awen's fifth calf that May; it would be a good strong one if her other calves were anything to go by, and I had already decided that if it was a heifer I would keep it for ourselves, and have her in the herd for breeding.

That morning I knew something was wrong, a cow was missing. Everyone was together contentedly grazing the fresh spring grass - except one; always it is the first sign for any stockman that there is trouble, because very rarely does a member of a herd wander too far from the rest. No one was expected to calve for at least 3 or 4 weeks, so that would not account for a missing cow, for that is one of the rare times when they do go off to be by themselves, when they are about to calve. Quickly I looked over the beasts and soon discovered it was Awen who was absent. Next was the searching along the hedgerows of the field; for it is in a corner or close to a hedge a sick animal will take itself off, as we might take ourselves to our beds for shelter and comfort away from others who might bother us.

Soon my searching was over; she was standing at the far end of the field, head hung in great dejection, not eating, not cudding, no lifting of the head as I approached. Such a lovely beast transformed into a wreck in a matter of hours. Whatever it was, was having a terrible effect on her, and if something wasn't done quickly, she would next go down, and all could be lost.

Within an hour we had her in the pen and the vet was busy examining her, no need for a tether, for the sickness had taken away any strength she might have had to resist, and it is that those who depend on us for their feeding and care, do so even more in their time of illness; and their hallow eyes search us for help, hoping that we might release them from their lowness.

"Dead calf", said the vet as he withdrew his hand from inside the big cow "Beginning to smell a bit too, so she has been like it for a few days, and will be setting up an infection by now. We'll have to get it off her"-

Dead calf, so why? This would be her 5th, we've never had trouble with Awen before", I said, feeling very depressed about my best cow. "Anyone's guess at the moment", replied the young vet, "we'll get a blood test – that should throw some light on it. Better tie her up, this is going to be a bit of a struggle. Don't think she'll be helping us much in her state, and with a dead calf inside too - she will probably go down, so give her plenty of rope", he said as he climbed the gate and made for the back of his car for the calving aid.

Calving aids can be tractors with ropes, which are vicious and can cause a lot of problems, pully blocks, or the latest invention, which is a long steel bar with a cross beam on one end which fits against the rear of the cow, while the other end jams into the ground, its length is made up of a ratchet, on which is fixed a lever and calving ropes to go round the unborn calf's front feet. The beauty of this machine is that it pulls the calf gently out from the cow in a downward direction, but can still, even so, be very hard work and tricky too, if the cow goes down. Always there is the risk of the poor animal haemorrhaging and dying instantly.

When I was a lad, and working at my first job on a dairy farm, we had a terrible time with a batch of maiden heifers. The boss cursed the day he bought a particular bull; for there was always trouble with the young heifers calving, because the bull caused them to have such big calves. All during that autumn we had heifers having difficult calvings. Some mornings we would find a sad little heifer standing next to the cold lifeless body of her calf; gazing down at it in bewilderment, wondering why it wasn't responding to her soft lowings and gentle lickings. It is such times as this when I find it hardest to manage my feelings over these poor simple creatures.

My greatest shock during that time though was at the calving of another. Generally my boss was never happy to have a vet, for it was heavy money they cost, so always we had to try ourselves to put the problems right, and that is how it was on that occasion. With the pulling of two big men on the calving ropes for some long while, still the calf would not be freed from its young mother. And so the tractor was brought, a rope tied at the back, and the other end to the unfortunate little unborn calf inside the exhausted heifer lying there on the ground.

It was soon over. The tractor's strength far outweighed the two burly men, the calf was born amongst gushing rivers of blood, and within seconds the brave little heifer had followed the calf into the blessed relief and rest of death. In my mind I have never forgotten the events of that day, and I have always told myself since, that the heavy money which I have to pay for a vet is far less weight on the mind, than the guilt of living with a death, which I may have prevented, had I been prepared to get the best help.

I was not at ease with our Awen, I never did like these difficult calvings; there was so much that could go wrong, already we had lost the calf; would we be losing our best cow today too?

The young vet was ready, and he carefully slid his hand, with the calving rope inside the cow, it would not be easy, for he would be having to work by feel, trying to place the rope over the calf's foot using just one hand and everything would be tight, and the dead calf would be a long way down in the cow's womb, for she was not expected to calve for another three or four weeks. After a long tense silence, pushing and twisting, the first rope was in place – and then the second followed in the same laborious way.

"Now for it", murmured the vet under his breath. The calving aid in place, and fixed to the two ropes protruding from the cow, he slowly primed the ratchet to take up the slack. "Lean on her, and keep her against the side of the pen, but be ready if she goes down", he instructed. He swung on the lever, pushing it forward and dragging it back. Slowly it moved down the geared steel pole, forward and back, straining the ropes as it went. After what seemed an age, the calf's two front feet emerged. Awen moved uneasily from side to side, and the vet struggled on; harder it became, as the legs were drawn through and the nose appeared. The head by now was pressing its way against the narrow opening. "I thought it seemed big, when I felt it inside", he gasped. The cow feeling the movement of her calf tried to help, but she was too weak with the infection, and her contractions too were not spontaneous. The swinging of the lever became more and more difficult, as the weight of the calf's head and then its shoulders forced their way from the cow. "She's going down", I murmured, and I watched as the legs crumpled from under our best cow, and her huge form fell to the floor of the pen.

The young vet quickly repositioned the calving aid against a post. With nimble hand he readjusted the ratchet back up the pole from its place at the bottom where the long drag had taken it. "Sit on her and try and keep her still", he commanded; I obeyed immediately, and he continued with his slog. By now the front end of the lifeless calf was hanging from the cow, and leaving the rib cage to present the next problem. Not only was the cow exhausted, the young vet was beginning to flag too, but he rejected my offer to take over from him. He felt responsible, and would take things through to the end, whatever that might mean.

At times like these, there is always great tenseness in the air – no one speaks – only what they have to, for the mind needs all its concentration, and never might anyone know when the point of no return has arrived; only do we know when it has passed with the flooding of her blood. But a vet needs always to be a gambling man, and he will weigh up in his own mind the risks of taking a particular course; but life being the way we find it, a weighting of the mind still will leave doubts, and never, until the calf is clear of its dam, and it can be seen that all is right with both, will minds be relaxed once again.

With more straining on the lever, the rib cage of the calf broke free from the cow, and quickly and silently the wet black little body slid to the ground. The birth was over. Awen was safe and free of that which should have brought her the happiness and delight of pleasure, but had instead taken her close to death. And as that little form lay there on the ground so innocent and still and lifeless, I knelt down beside her and pondered, "The life she never saw."

CHAPTER 7

Some Bulls I Have Known

"Never trust a bull" is probably one of the best-known agricultural sayings ever coined; yet one of the least acknowledged. Endless stories of maimings and killings litter our history. Even so, a lot depends on the breed, or how he was reared, how he is treated, which side of the bed he got out that morning, who he is running with, what is happening around him at any given time; if there is a threat from anyone or thing; and it helps greatly, right from the start to form a rapport, as much as you are able, so that he can trust you.

In the early days we used to hire a bull; generally to put on our Hereford x Friesian cows. They were always co-operative, although we did have a bit of trouble with one.

He'd been running with the cows for about seven weeks (we like to keep them for about nine weeks if we can). A cow comes on bulling roughly every three weeks, so by keeping the bull for that length of time there is a better chance of getting everyone in calf.

One day I noticed the bull was lying down by himself, and the cows were nowhere to be seen. The following day it was the same, but when I did discover the cows at the other end of the hill, there was one bulling. My first instincts of the previous day were confirmed; there was something wrong with this bull, otherwise why wasn't he right here in the midst of the action?

But as I stood watching the cows I noticed this little black creature jumping about amongst them. "We haven't got anything all black or that small," I thought. Suddenly it dawned on me. A chap whose farm is about 2 miles away, but who happened to rent a field adjoining the hill, believe it or not, had just turned his suckler herd, and a bull into that field. Not only was this downright irresponsible, for he would have known we had a bull running at the time, and if the two had met, there would have been fireworks, because our Charolais, (had he been fit would probably have killed this little Aberdeen Angus). Which as it turned out had been borrowed from this chap's brother-in-law. So I reckon the brother-in-law would have probably killed him too.

Anyway, this little twerp of a bull had jumped the fences and served one of the cows. But I didn't want an Aberdeen Angus cross calf out of one of my cows; it would be too blooming small compared with a Charolais cross, and I wouldn't get much of a price for it.

Sure enough, as it turned out, when I did come to sell that batch of store cattle over two years later; the result of this clandestine relationship was about 60 quid less than for any of the rest. And I don't think I ever did get the money back from his N.F.U. insurance either.

Fortunately for both of us, after this exercise in forging good relationships between neighbours he whipped the lot of them out of the field a bit smartish.

I still have this funny feeling though, every time I think about what happened. Whether by putting his cows in the field next to my Charolais bull, he was in fact hoping that my big bull would be the one to jump the fences – not his. After all, twenty cows multiplied by an extra £60 was £1200.

The other curious thing about this business was that when later I came to check the fences, to make sure his bull hadn't broken any of them down in his bid for a bit on the side, I discovered that maybe he hadn't been quite so amorous as I first thought. Because as it turned out, the local badger population, who were busy building a sett close to our boundary fence, had neatly piled the spoil from the excavations right over and across the fence; making a very convenient and gently sloping ramp, which judging from the footprints, this Angus bull had used for his escape, and night out.

Which left us still with a very sick Charolais bull, who would need to be returned to his owner; and did he take some handling to get down from the hill and loaded into the lorry? Poor chap, he was obviously feeling very unwell and irritable, because soon afterwards he was diagnosed as having kidney failure, and had to be put down.

The experience of that stroppy bull reminds me of my youth. At the time I was working as an assistant cowman – No, I mean a cowman's assistant – to a largish Friesian herd, (for those days fifty milkers was large).

Dairy bulls are generally seen to be more aggressive than beef bulls; and the Jersey bull is the worst of the lot.

In this particular herd there was a delightful old cow called Glamour; she was gentle and extremely well behaved, easily spotted because she was practically white all over. The boss decided that the little practically-white-all-over-too, calf she had just produced would make a good bull; so we wouldn't castrate him, and we would keep him penned up in the calf pens where he would be always in close contact with people; get more handling and, hopefully, grow into a fine quiet beast like his mother.

Unbeknown to us, until much later, that was; the farm, being too close to the local council estate for its own good; caused us, on occasions to get visits from some of the young inmates from there; and over the following months these little blighters used to secretly get into the calf pens, and wind-up this young bull by practising their matadorial skills on him.

Soon it became obvious to those of us who were responsible for his well-being; that we had here a beast who was remarkably aggressive for his age; and completely at odds with his mother's temperament. It was by now no longer possible to even venture into the pen to feed him; because he would immediately attack you; and we all began to wonder about the wisdom of keeping him. Nevertheless, the boss had made up his mind, and wasn't about to change it.

By the time we discovered the reason for the animal's aggressiveness, he was old enough to be used on the heifers, and whenever we needed to move him about the farm, it was an exercise in the most detailed tactical logistics that even the British army couldn't have matched.

Never was he to be driven, because he would simply turn right round on you. The method was to open doors and gates in the general direction in which you wanted him to travel, blocking all other exits off with tractors, or whatever else was to hand; and the most important rule of all – to keep well hidden and right out of sight. The chap who had to open the gate of the pen, after everything else was ready, had to make sure he had an absolutely clear means of escape in the opposite direction. He had to be young and agile so as to jump as quickly as possible, all the walls and gates, as he had time for, to get the maximum distance between the bull and himself.

The trick was, at the same time, to have within a relatively short distance, and within easy eyesight, the reason for all these tactics, which was generally, a bunch of bulling heifers. Whereupon, as soon as he had spotted them, you knew your problems were over. For without any more gazing about for a likely human target; and with his head set, and his eye marked, he would trot on at great speed, straight at the heifers, whimpering with delight.

From then on it was an easy exercise to move the whole lot into whichever field you wanted them to be; he of course, by then would be completely pre-occupied sniffing around all those fresh young gals.

We always reckoned, even with this young tyrant that if he was amongst heifers he wasn't a threat to anyone else. Of course, it had to be me to blow this myth right out of the water didn't it?

I had just finished a length of hedge trimming with a long handled hook in the field of stubble next to where he and some heifers happened to be. Being pre-occupied with my work, I hadn't noticed that as I slowly progressed along my side of the hedge; watching closely and progressing, just as slowly and deliberately along the other side was he himself. By the time I had reached the gate, which was as far as I had to go, he had clear sight of me; and only then did I realise what had been going on.

Suddenly, to his delight, did he realise too, that there was nothing more between the two of us than a tubular steel gate, resting on the ground, and tied to the posts on either side at the top, with bits of barbed wire. Not noticing immediately the flimsiness of the situation between us, I began to walk directly away from the gate, across the stubble ground, towards the farm. On glancing back over my shoulder, I was a bit shocked to see that the wretched animal, either by chance, or by calculated evil, had by now got his head on the ground, and was starting to lift the bottom of the gate off the ground. Whereupon it was gently slipping up over his head and beginning to travel back along his neck.

I never reckoned I was much of a runner, and there was probably 300 yards between me and the gate on the other side of the field – "anyway chum," I thought, "you don't run from a bull unless you've got at least a 1000 to one chance. So do I stand and wait until he's slipped the gate up his neck and along over his back and walked out and, as he advances on me, slice him to bits with my 'hedging hook?' I didn't even think of that stupid idea, (it was just some fantasy I had later), because there was no time to think; just to walk quickly and directly back to what was by now the near horizontal gate, hanging on a puzzled bull, who couldn't quite work out how to handle a gate in this unusual position.

Having got back to him, I then turned, and began walking up the hedge again; whereupon the dafty beggar promptly dropped the gate and followed me along on the other side of the hedge. Getting a fair way up along the hedge from the gate I then set out at right angles from it, across the field, and to my relief, on looking back saw that he hadn't the sense to rush back down to the gate, and have another bash at it. But instead stood quite contentedly, where he was, peering over the hedge, as I disappeared off into the distance.

Like so many dairy farms at that time and since, reliable labour, happy to get out of bed half way through the night, and spend a large chunk of most days throughout the year tied to a cow's tail for peanuts for pay, was hard to come by.

By now the cowman had left, and I had been milking the cows on my own; and soon I would be off to the local farm institute. Called colleges these days; for everyone and everything are no longer what they really are; but have to pretend to the world to be something better. Nothing, or no one, is any longer allowed to be left at the bottom of the social pile, it seems.

Having to face up to the stark reality of my leaving, and no one prepared to take on the job; unfortunately the boss had only one option, and that was to sell the herd.

I don't remember much about all the preparation for the sale day, although I suppose there must have been some. The chances are, that knowing things on that place, there would have been very little, and what there was, would have been left to the last minute.

The sale ring was to be erected by the auctioneers men in one of the yards, so that would certainly have to be cleaned out.

Set in a slight valley, I imagine for shelter, the collecting and loafing yards for the cows were on either side of the milking parlour. (Collecting yard: where the cows stood before milking; and loafing yard: where they waited after being milked, for the rest to be). Although the buildings were fairly sheltered from the wind, they weren't from the wet. Every track leading to the farm served as a riverbed during a rainy spell. That was fine, if the drains were, because they just fed the surface water off into the stream, which had been culverted along under the farm buildings, keeping all the yards dry – in theory.

But, of course, where you have animals, you have dung and the cows standing about for several hours during the day, before and after morning and evening milking, produced a heck of a lot of dung; and mixed with water produces masses and masses of slurry, and slurry blocks drains – if you don't watch out. So always, especially in winter these yards looked like large murky lagoons, because no one bothered to watch out. Naturally, in the end you were forced to do something with all this brown, greenish stuff, because if you didn't, it would take over, and the buildings would become flooded with it.

The sale then, was a good reason to get stuck in with drain rods, brushes and shovels; and as many chaps as there were, were recruited into loading what they could onto trailers, and slurping the rest down the drains into the underground stream, and off down the valley to – I never really knew where; and I don't think anyone else did either. But no one from down the valley ever complained. That was O.K. in those days, but today would be different, with heavy fines and threats of imprisonment for river pollution on a grand scale like this, or even on any scale, no matter how small. So don't get peeing, or cleaning your nose out down a drain anymore, because they'll catch you; the men with the bottles and test tubes – they'll catch you!

Sloshing about in slurry can be boring, so when, after morning milking there was a heifer to be put to the bull, everyone was happy to assist. The heifer was driven into the service race and crushed up to hold her still. The bull was then released from his pen, where he then promptly moved smartly along the race towards the back end of the heifer. Quickly, heaving his front onto her back, he gave a sharp little hop with his rear legs, and the job was done. Everyone back to the boring old slurry slurping again.

But John Spence had other ideas. Spence was a lad of about fifteen, Irish extraction, and came from the local council estate; he had a delightful inoffensive nature, and wasn't averse to the occasional prank. He could have fitted in quite easily amongst a bunch of horse dealers with his stocky build, ready smile and gruff Irish, Gloucestershire lilt.

"Leave her in John", he shouted across the yard to me, referring to the still penned up heifer. "I'll ride her round the yard" – Just as easily as that, it seemed; and as if she were a well-schooled pony, saddled up and ready for a morning's canter. Everyone's drainrods, shovels and brushes, which just a minute before had been taken up again, were put smartly back down. All eyes were turned on Spence as he began wading his way, unconcernedly through the slurry across to the young cow, who for the minute anyway was quite content to stand quietly, reflecting on the events of the past few minutes.

Being Irish, I suppose, allows you to do most things which others wouldn't consider, so everyone knew that this wasn't just some idle talk, but really was about to happen. Even so, did he really think he could stay on the back of this young animal? I imagine he did. So the 9" deep sea of slurry still covering the yard wouldn't be a problem. Having stayed on, how did he propose stopping this cavorting animal so that he could get off? The answer to that must be, he obviously intended staying on until the beast grew tired and stopped with exhaustion.

All we hoped for now, was that the boss wouldn't put in an appearance before the entertainment began. If he happened to come after Spence had mounted the beast, and the crush gate had been opened, the show would have to go on, unimpeded, despite his presence. No doubt he would bellow

Spence's name across the yard, which would probably have the effect of unnerving him, and bringing the event to an abrupt halt; and we would all be in dead trouble for aiding and abetting. But so far, so good; the boss wasn't in sight.

The easy bit was to climb onto the wall of the race, and then, a more tricky bit, to softly lower himself onto the heifer's back without upsetting her. With much gentle talk he managed this. The heifer started fidgeting; but with nowhere to go; the high walls on either side; a steel gate to her rear, and another to her front; she eventually settled down once more. Spence made himself comfortable, and with his nerve obviously still firmly under control, he whispered: "Now" – and the gate was opened.

For a moment, silence descended over the place; the heifer remained motionless with Spence waiting, poised for the ride of his life. Everyone else stood still, not daring to move for fear of sloshing the slurry and unnerving the beast; for we knew we must get this absolutely right; and by now anyway, we had all convinced ourselves that this was really going to happen. – Spence was sitting there, calm – and he would conquer this animal – What was to stop him? – He had got this far, and - He would do what he said he would!

Suddenly, realising her way was no longer barred, and without any warning; the heifer sprang forth, out of the crush. Taking two or three leaps across the yard. Whereupon Spence left her company and was immediately half submerged and prostrate in the slurry; whilst she galloped on, heels kicking, triumphant with glee, and realising that it was she, after all, who had been the conqueror.

Having eventually cleaned up the yard, and successfully secreted Spence away for the rest of that day, in case the boss saw the state of him and thought he had been mucking about; things began to move forward quite rapidly towards the sale day.

The auctioneer had already catalogued the stock, complete with their pedigree, names and ear numbers; from the very smallest calf, through to the young heifers, steers, and onto the milkers: with the elderly cows and bulls; which were to be sold last.

When the day eventually arrived, the sale was scheduled to start at 10.30am after morning milking, so that the purchasers could get their animals home in time for the evening milking on their own places.

The farm began to fill with people, and cars were set out in neat rows in the front field, with a couple of lads acting as car park attendants, kitted out in white coats, which gave them an uncanny air of authoritative distinctiveness. The young calves were in the calf pens which had been by now all bedded up with unusually large quantities of bright clean straw; so vast were the quantities, that in some cases it was difficult to discover the sleeping occupants amongst it. We had all realised very quickly that today was about top show, and impressiveness. And we were all soon swept along with the magical atmosphere of the occasion – keen to make things look as good as possible, despite the shockingly dilapidated state of the buildings all around us.

Never mind, they were all here to view the stock. Although as I mingled amongst the crowd it was plain to see, that many of the local faces I recognised were here for a nose, because as everyone knew, most of them never had the price of a pint of beer between them.

The yearling heifers and steers were yarded together; once again in hock-deep straw as were the cows, who were obviously enjoying this unheard-of luxury. For always it was, from the boss "you're using too much straw for bedding – it won't last the winter". So that by the time you had got to the far end of the shed, forking it about like spreading war-time butter on your bread during the rationing, you wondered where it had all gone, especially after some of the cows had taken to grazing it off, as a bit of a change from the usual silage, and others had decided to have a skittish chase about; the skim of clean straw was pretty well threadbare again.

As the stock stood, or lay about, relaxed and apparently completely unaware of all the activity around them. Each by now with their own personalised, two red and white, oval numbers slapped on either side of their backs with thick brown glue, and which hopefully tallied with the sale catalogue. People began to drift to the calf pens where the auctioneer was to begin.

After the introductory formalities and the flamboyant description of the herd and farm, which those of us who laboured there each day, had great difficulty in recognising, the auctioneer began the long process of grinding through what seemed endless lots. By the time the calves were sold, everyone then filed through out into the yard and collected about the sale ring; from where the proceedings continued, with the selling of the older animals. First the steers, and then onto the heifers, most of which were easily recognised as their mothers daughters.

It was only then that I suddenly became aware of what we were all doing here today. We were parting with the life-blood of the farm – the livestock of the place. After today there would be no animals, other than the dogs left here. I had never known these buildings, or the fields about them without living creatures. This would mean that instead, all the grassland would be ploughed up and sown down to cereals or potatoes. And as the proceedings wore on I became increasingly, more and more despondent.

By now the milking cows were being brought through from the sheds where they had spent every winter of their lives sheltering from the elements; the sheds, which for them had been home, and which, unbeknown to them, they would, after today, never be seeing again.

As face after familiar face was brought into the ring to present to the buyers; individual faces, individual markings, even individual udders, I could recognise because of the closeness of a cowman to his charges, as he milked them twice every day, practically every day of each year.

Eventually, the bidding came to an end. The show was over, the last beast left the ring, and those who had been successful in their bids made themselves busy loading their new purchases onto the waiting lorries. As soon as each lorry was ready, and the buyers had satisfied the auctioneer's clerk, they set off down the 1/4 mile long, rough track leading from the farm. The dust enveloping them as they went, until both dust and distance separated them and their bewildered cargoes, from us forever.

As I walked back into the silent yard, which only a short time before was bustling with human and animal life, standing there, was one solitary lorry, its tailgate down, and reversed against the steel gate of the bull pen. From the top front ventilator behind the driver's cab a rope reached out, with its end on the ground beneath. Inside the lorry, it trailed back along the bed and down the open rear where its end stopped at the bullpen gate. Although there was no sign of the infamous white bull, I knew he must be there in the pen somewhere. From within the buildings I was faintly aware of the murmur of low voices engaged in what appeared to be anxious discussion.

At that moment, the boss called me from up at the house. It was about an hour later by the time I returned. The lorry had gone and so had the white bull. Someone had bought him. Whether they had been tipped off before they had done so, or whether they had discovered it for themselves, after they had, I never found out. Whichever way it happened, they were a couple of brave men, with a lot of tactical ingenuity, judging by that rope. But how did they manage to get the bull from his pen, and along the service race to the steel gate, where they could tie the rope through his ring; without having a cow to draw him there? And even when they had succeeded in doing this, and managed to entice him into the lorry by leading him with the rope, pulled from outside, at the front, how would they handle him again at the other end, by which time he would probably be pretty wound up with the journey, still with about 40ft. of rope hanging from his nose and none of the confinement of a crush to release it, only the empty lorry, which he had all to himself, and I reckon there would be no one on this earth who would have a chance of controlling him?

Over the years, I've met some pretty wily stockmen, able to outwit most animals. Perhaps this was a couple of them. Or maybe, they were just a bit Irish like Spence.

Most beef breeding systems, and certainly the one we were running rely on free ranging all of the time, all day long, and all the year round, with only an outside handling pen and crush for such times as testing for T.B., medical treatment, difficult calving, and for loading, when the young stock would need to be leaving the place. Otherwise, feeding, mating, normal births, and suckling the calves is all done on the hoof -What is known as "dog and stick farming;" or low-input-low-output farming, with relatively low capital costs. But to achieve all of that you do need the right breed to meet the criterion; and if you ain't going to house them during the winter like we didn't, because you couldn't afford the cost of that housing, then the only type of beast capable of coping comfortably with persistent bad weather will be one of the old traditional hardy British hill breeds.

So when we eventually decided we must have our own bull because of the problems we were facing at the time with hiring one, it was to Wales we again looked, where several years before we had bought all our pedigree foundation cows.

A good bull is essential, because his influence will determine the quality of the offspring from the whole herd. Tracking down that bull is not always easy, but generally the best place to start, is to seek out the advice of those people you have already dealt with, and bought heifers from. That is the breeders of the black cattle of Wales. Soon we had got a name, it was of a respected and well-known breeder from a village just north of Aberystwyth. Many times, over the years I had noticed at the pedigree sales his stock often fetched some of the best prices, so that seemed a very good idea; and sure enough, he had a young bull available at the right time, at what seemed a reasonable price.

Fortunately or unfortunately, depending on how you looked at it, my mother had died of old age twelve months earlier, and left us a small legacy, so I had no qualms at all in using some of it to buy a bull, otherwise I know we would have been hard pressed to find the funds, and I know too, because of her prudent nature, and interest in the cattle, my mother would rather have known that the money was going into something that hopefully might help generate income, than see it sunk into something, for example, like a smart new car, which would sooner or later have rotted away.

Having spoken on the phone and confirmed the asking price with John Rees, the owner of the bull, (every other man in Wales seems to be a John Rees), a few days later Pat and I set off to have a look at the animal for ourselves. When we eventually arrived, for our journeys into Wales are always slow and interesting, we were given the usual warm welcome, as on all these cattle buying expeditions; and as usual, instantly knew it was very genuine; not just because they were hoping to part us from our money, but because of great desire to be helpful and to please. Mr. Rees was not going to manipulate the proceedings in any way. "Will you have a look at him first," he said, "and then we can come and have something to eat after that. Or would you rather do it the other way round?" We agreed to the first suggestion and, picking up his stick, he led us to a shed, and in we went to inspect our prospective purchase.

The bull was barely 12 months old, but a reasonable size for his age- not too big and fat, for that is always a sure sign of a beast "caked up" on expensive feed, which at worse could cause him to be infertile, and would anyway make him lose condition once he was fed on basic grass and hay, which he most certainly would be back at our place. It was obvious he had been handled a lot, he moved around obligingly as he was gently persuaded, so that we were able to see how he walked and what he looked like from all directions. "A nice looking animal, and very quiet", I commented, not being an expert, although I suppose I wasn't completely clueless, but at the same time wouldn't care to argue with a judge in a show ring; and here, anyway was an honest man with a reputation to protect, so I felt I was on fairly safe ground. Mr. Rees just nodded in agreement with our comments, and occasionally offered up remarks in his soft Welsh voice.

Having farmed for some time at Brysgagga, and past retirement age, John Rees and his wife had moved from the farm house to a modern bungalow nearby to make room for his son and family. Even so, he still had an enormous interest in cattle breeding, and brought a wealth of experience to the job. "Do you think you will have him then?" he said eventually. We said we would, and fixed a date two months hence, when we would collect him, with an adjustment in the price for the extra time he would be on their farm.

After paying a deposit, and sitting down round the table with the family for a proper tea; and then having been invited to look round the farm at the other stock, so as to be assured of their high quality, we set off back home, happy that we had spent a very rewarding and worthwhile day,

Two months later, at the end of July we returned again, this time with the livestock trailer behind the car. In that short time the bull had grown noticeably, and began to look as though he might now manage to live up to the rather grand sounding name of Brysgagga Erddyn 9th. John Rees son led him out of the shed on a halter, (which he said, he had just recently started training him to), and straight into the trailer, as if he had been doing it every day of his life, the tailgate was shut, and the young Erddyn stood there patiently waiting for whatever was to happen next. So as to give ourselves plenty of time for mishaps on the journey back, we set straight off after paying the balance of the money. "He hasn't seen any females since he was weaned from his mother", said John Rees, "so he'll have a nice surprise at the other end when he sees your ladies", and with that we drove out of the yard.

An hour or so into our journey we stopped in a quiet spot for some lunch, and to inspect our purchase. He was obviously enjoying the new experience, as he was just contentedly lying down there amongst the straw; and later, when we stopped again for a cup of tea, I had another look, and felt he hadn't moved an inch since I last looked in at him.

The journey home took about four and a half hours, we arrived by late afternoon. The plan was to drive up, and right out onto the hill, hoping that the cows would all be hanging about there, or at least somewhere within sight of the bull as we unloaded him, which would of course make life much easier for us. As we drove from the track, through the gate onto the open grassland of the top of the hill, nowhere was a cow to be seen, certainly not close at hand, and as we looked around towards the far end, there were none there either. "They must be down at the water trough", I murmured to Pat. The water trough being a good quarter of a mile away at the bottom of the hill, and well out of sight until you were very nearly upon it. "Well, I hope we can manage to drive him alright" she replied. After all, he didn't know us, and we didn't know him, so it would be anyone's guess as to how he would behave. With a last look round in the other direction, along the banks, where it is easy for a whole herd of cattle to be concealed amongst the folds in the hillside, we satisfied ourselves that they weren't there either, so there was no chance of an easy option, and we had just better get on with it, and hope for the best.

The thing in our favour was that the chap was still lying down quite happily in the trailer, even though it had been stationary for the last 15 minutes. "He is either extremely docile, or half dead" I said- "Let's hope it's the first thing". By now I had dropped the tailgate expecting him to get up and walk out - which he didn't. Well, I wasn't going to get myself in there with him, prodding about to set him on his feet in case, having got myself cornered, he turned nasty; so the poking was done through the side inspection door, as I stood outside. Eventually this had the desired effect, and he slowly lifted himself onto his feet, and after much stretching, ambled down the ramp onto the grass. The two of us promptly took up our positions with stout sticks at his rear, and gently moved him forward in the direction to which we hoped the cows had gone.

Dogs have their place with stock, and if a beast is not used to them they are more trouble than good, and the animal you are trying to persuade to co-operate will often spend its time ignoring you, and having a go at the dog instead, which it sees as a threat. So Bryn stayed firmly shut in the car.

To get animals to do as you want them in an open space, as we were there, is more often an exercise in gentle persuasion. They have to want to do as you want them to: because if they don't - then they won't - and you've lost the battle before you've even begun; and they will just take off; and you might as well go home and forget it. So it had to be with this lad. Just quiet words, and keeping firmly up behind him, but all the time, at the ready in case he suddenly thought he had had enough of all this, and quickly turned round and sorted us out. The pace was fairly brisk, and quite comfortable, he stayed on the track, and on the odd occasion when he was tempted to wander off it, he allowed himself to be easily nudged back again

We were almost, by now, at a point above where we thought the cows would be, when as he went by, he took a quick whiff at a fresh cow pat, standing there, all by itself, on the track. Now to you and me all cow pats look and smell roughly about the same, within reason anyway: but obviously not to him, because, without even a second sniff, his pace quickened rapidly, and as he trotted forward, the whining started, and the whining turned to grumbling, and the grumbling to growling, and as he came to an open piece of flat grass, the growling became louder, and louder, and soon it was a roar, which also became louder and louder, until I thought we must have all been transformed to some darkest African jungle, with the sound reverberating off the hills around us.

As he cantered onto the flat area of grass, with the noise becoming more and more blood curdling, he suddenly stopped and turned to face us, putting his head to the ground, he began pawing it. "Quick"! I whispered to Pat, "he's going to charge - "Dive behind the bushes – Out of sight: out of mind". As we scrambled in amongst the clumps of hawthorn and holly the noise receded, and peering out, we could see that his attention had by now been taken from us, and he was concentrating on the airborne scents, wafting up from below, where the cows and calves were lying about by the water trough enjoying the afternoon warmth. By now we were in a position amongst the bushes to be able to see both him, and look down on them.

As if they had all been jabbed with some sort of electric probe, the calves were on their feet and racing up the hill towards the mighty sound. The cows, who normally are more reluctant to get themselves raised were close behind; and as the natives met the intruder on that hillside, the hustle and bustle, and the sniffing and smelling that quickly followed, took over and settled the tenseness of the wild anxious moments of before; and the peace of that summer afternoon returned once again.

As we walked back across the hill towards the trailer, I did wonder what we had let ourselves in for, and then I remembered John Rees's words as we had driven out of his yard, "He hasn't seen a female since he was weaned from his mother" - and I thought - "Well, who can blame him for his misbehaviour on this occasion?" - and thank goodness, it was just on this occasion: for ever since then he has been the same placid, calm, gentle, good natured beast that he was on the first day we saw him.

Strange the effect women have on men though, isn't it?

CHAPTER 8

A Funny Thing Happened To
Me On The Way To . . . .

Most people who have even a slight interest in farming will have heard of the Belted Galloway: But by contrast over the years I have met no one outside of the farming fraternity of Wales, who has ever heard of Belted Welsh.

Unfortunately for the Welsh, anyone who does catch sight of a belted animal, even in Wales will automatically assume they are looking at a Galloway; and so the Scotch myth that all belted cattle come from that other place is perpetuated.

Running a few of these beasts ourselves was something we decided upon at an early stage in the transition to Welsh cattle. The belted beast is of course the same as the black one, apart from its colour, so it is quite a simple matter to run the two types together, using either a belted bull or a black bull on both types of cow. The belt being dominant is useful because it does allow you to run a pedigree black bull, so keeping your pedigree black cattle pure; and at the same time, more often than not, producing a belted calf from a belted cow. When this occurs, because of the shortage of the belted stock it is perfectly allowable to register (provided it is well marked) the offspring of this union with the other Welsh cattle society: Gwartheg Hynafol Cymru. (The Ancient Cattle of Wales). This society, despite its name, only came into being in 1981; and was formed to cover and protect all the other coloured cattle of Wales which also included the white, line backed, blue, red and smokey, which were fast disappearing from the face of Wales. Even so, as a society it is still struggling to survive and keep alive some of the old traditional colours of Welsh cattle.

The problem of the lost colours started in 1904 when a breed society was formed which accepted just black as the standard colour, and so from then on, the other colours went into rapid decline; only saved by the few most ardent of the Welsh cattle breeders who weren't prepared to have what must have been generations of work wiped away because of fashion: and a later problem of the 1930s: which was when the bull licensing law came into being. A law brought about by the Government, because of its concern for the decreasing quality of the national cattle herd, with the continuing practice of breeding, using any old bull, from any old place. This of course was a wise move, on the face of it: but London would not accept the registration of any Welsh bull, other than the Blacks, which of course meant that to use a bull of any of the other colours was illegal.

Naturally, no self respecting Welsh farmer was going to be told what he was allowed to do, or not do by London if he could possibly avoid it, especially if it interfered with a long Welsh family tradition. The answer, therefore, was simple. – Don't let the snoopers find your bull – Hide him from the prying eyes of the inspectors by keeping him up the mountain.

It is to those good patriotic chaps that today we owe the survival of the other Welsh cattle colours. Of course the situation is different now. No longer do we have the bull licensing scheme, so all those hidden away bulls are legal once again, and have long come out of hiding.

Despite this change, as younger generations come on, even in Wales, many of the new breeders have, over the years infiltrated their Welsh cattle herds with faster maturing stock from foreign places, notably Europe, which produces beef pretty well about the same flavour and texture as the pap from a broiler chicken. – So what do you expect if you grow an animal stuffed full of concentrates in 18 months, instead of feeding it on silage or hay and grass, and waiting for 30 months for it to mature? But then, try feeding the pampered continental breeds on only grass and you will find they soon wilt away. As for the economics of the exercise – of course time is money, and if you can produce 3 crops of beef in the time it takes you to make 2 crops, then that looks good, but the feed lorry does keep turning up at the gate with frightening regularity. Biased or not, an awful lot of what appears to be commercial decisions are taken purely because of fashion, or wanting to be seen as progressive.

Anyway: despite all the odds loaded against us, the Ancient Cattle of Wales struggles on, and believe it or not, when we applied, several years ago, to the Rare Breeds Survival Trust for membership, they refused us, because, in their words. "Your breed society hadn't been in existence long enough" – So, because no one had bothered to form a breed society for all those different Welsh coloured beasts until 1981, that meant the cattle didn't exist either, did it? That sounds to me like the brilliantly logical thinking of a top ranking civil servant. Fortunately for all sane people, the one who responded in this way to our request for membership has now lost his iron grip on the Trust, and the feelings are that we would now be allowed to join. But then, whether rightly or wrongly, we decided, after that snub, to go it alone, the thinking being – if you join the Trust as a rare breed, sooner or later, because of the high profile you achieve, the rarity value is very often lost.

So instead we just try and hang onto things.

"Will you be going to the AGM", asked Megan Pughe on the other end of the phone. We had hired the Pughe's belted bull for a few weeks to put him on our Belts and four of the Black cattle to see what would happen. As it turned out, from the four Blacks we had put him to, one didn't get in calf, one was completely black, and two had the most perfectly proportioned belts we have ever had since. Of course they had to be a couple of bull calves, and we weren't in a position to accommodate a full time bull, and I was unable to sell them on for breeding, so they unfortunately ended up on dinner plates. The only consolation was that I did a couple of water colours of them as calves, which we have hanging on the wall, and which we then turned into greeting cards; and fine looking calves they are too.

"Well yes", I said, replying to Megan's question. "I thought I could return your bull, and then go down to Dolgellau in time for the AGM in the evening, all at the same time."

"Could you take me down too" came the reply – "only Emlyn has had to go into hospital, so I have no way of getting down there this year". I hesitated for a moment, as I had originally intended to drop off the bull, go to the AGM and then get back home to Gloucestershire, all in one day, and it would have been pretty late by then anyway. So if I were to take Megan to Dolgellau as well I would then need to get her back home again, and that would be a round trip of at least 75 miles before I had even started off for home. Then suddenly I had a thought.

We had known Megan and Emlyn for sometime now because of our common interest in Belted Welsh cattle. On one occasion I had taken a friend, who was interested in buying some of their stock, up to have a look round their cattle; and despite having visited them on several occasions, they had always arranged to meet us on the moor, or some other remote, far flung place which they were grazing. One day they offered to give us lunch, and we ended up in a transport café.

All this did leave me rather puzzled, as to why we were never invited back to the house; and the more I thought about it, the more curious I became, with all sorts of pictures flitting through my mind; trying to visualise what it might be that they obviously didn't seem to want us to see. Well, I thought, now's my chance – and before fully realising it, I heard myself saying down the phone. "If you could put me up for the night, I can take you down and bring you back again, and then go home the next morning." To my surprise, and without any hesitation at all, the reply came back – that she would be only too pleased. For the next few days, I must admit, I did wonder what I had let myself in for.

We kept Rhidian, their Belted bull until the beginning of October. The arrangement was that I was to take him back onto the moor where I had collected him two months earlier; from a pen up there where he could be more easily loaded into the trailer. But this time I was to turn him loose after unloading him, and then to make my way down to the Pughes' house, having taken directions and instructions from Megan over the phone.

I suppose an extra 1500 feet, and a few degrees to the north of our place makes a difference to how the weather is, especially at that time of the year. – Springs are later and winters sooner over there.

Having unloaded the bull, who had been perfectly well behaved for the whole of the trip, and during his stay with us; I was feeling rather sad as I watched him walk from the trailer and trot off towards a bunch of cows in the distance of that grey afternoon. The whole operation was a bit uncanny really, because on the two occasions; both the collecting and the returning of the bull, there was never anyone in evidence anywhere. Having followed the directions for his collection, I arrived at the field, and sure enough, there standing in the pen, completely by himself was Rhidian, just as if he had been spirited there. I felt a bit like the disciples must have when Jesus told them where to find the colt he was to ride on through Jerusalem: only they were challenged when they untied it. Whereas, it was just the two of us, Rhidian and me: with not a sound, nor a sight of anyone for miles around – and, it was the same when I returned him.

"You're not expecting to take that trailer down there with you, are you?" was the curt reply I got when I stopped to ask, in the village, directions, to the Pughe's house, after unloading Rhidian on the moor. "Well, yes, I was hoping to. Do you think it will be a problem then?" I said. The local glanced along the length of the car and the livestock trailer behind it. "It might be alright." he said unconvincingly, and then directed me down, what could only be described as a steep concealed passage amongst the trees, running directly back and parallel to the road, and which I had already managed to pass three times without even noticing.

Autumns can be brilliant with their delightfully warm sunshine and beautiful shades of colours; but they can also be blooming grey, wet and depressing; and even when it is not raining, they can still be blooming grey wet and depressing. Today was the last sort.

After nearly turning the car upside down trying to get it aimed in the right direction, I began to make my way deeper and deeper down the concealed passage amongst the trees, where the greyness of the late damp autumn afternoon grew even deeper; and the valley into which I was secretly disappearing enveloped us: that is, the car and trailer and me (because by now I was beginning to feel that even these inanimate objects offered me some small crumb of comfort and consolation, amongst all the coldness of this place). The metalled road eventually wore out and disappeared altogether, giving way to holes, stones and water.

After what seemed the remainder of the day, the track righted itself, levelled out and began competing with the river, which by now was running beside it, or was meant to be. "At least I must be at the bottom of this place," I thought. "But where am I supposed to be going, and did the chap at the village really know what he was talking about, and if he didn't, and I'm in the wrong place, how am I ever going to turn this lot round and get back out again?" "And surely no one lives down here do they?"

After another few hundred yards, appearing through the gloom, I could just make out a Wellington boot – and – long macked-figure stumbling towards me, followed by a pack of assorted dogs. "I'm just going to shut these up for the night, and I'll be with you," shouted the long mac; which then made off towards an old abandoned car standing out from the trees at the side of the track; and opening the door, in the pack leapt.

"You found us then" said Megan's voice at the car window, peering out from the mac. "If you follow me, we'll sort things out, it's just along here"; and with that, off it went again. As the car lurched and splashed about between the ruts and holes, I was wondering when it was we were going to come into a clearing which could be a farmyard. Just then the mac turned and faced me. "Why have we stopped," I thought, and I realised then, that we had arrived.

To one side of the track the trees had given way a bit, to an assortment of rusting junk, most of which I couldn't recognise as any particular things. At the end of the track – because it was the end – just an end – not a finish with a turning space; was another battered old car, with lots of jumping barking figures silhouetted through the steamed-up windows- "Another kennel," I thought.

Then I noticed the house, which was standing squashed between the track and the wood behind it. Only it wasn't a house, it was an old ex holiday caravan, blue, I think, but green because of the moss and lichen.

Sitting still in the car for a while, I hoped that somehow or other, the mac would turn and carry on walking through a gap that might appear, which I hadn't noticed before, and we would arrive at something which could be a house, but it didn't; instead it walked back towards me.

"We'll have to hurry, or we'll be late for the meeting" she said.

Whether it hadn't dawned on her, I couldn't quite make out, but remembering what the chap back up in the village had said about. "Not expecting to take that trailer down there, are you?" – I wondered how we were going to turn the car, let alone the trailer as well.

"I reckon we'll have to unhitch the trailer, and manhandle it round, won't we?" I said at last. Now that too would be easier said than done, because even if we could squeeze the car back past the trailer when we had unhitched it, manhandling a 3/4 ton livestock trailer over all that rutty ground, which by now had a bit of an upward tilt on it, was going to be a little dodgy. However, after endless tugging, struggling and manipulating, we managed it. Again, after about a 14-point turn, I managed to get the car facing the other way too. I suppose my determination not to get trapped in this place a moment longer than I had to, enabled me to perform miracles that day; but despite my eagerness to get away, I knew, however I felt, that I would still be expected to take my hostess to the meeting; and then; as was agreed, stay the night as well. To do otherwise would be seen by her as a downright rejection of her hospitality; and that, despite this place, I didn't think I could ever do.

"I've got lots of extra food in," said Megan pointing to shelves of cereals and other groceries piled in the caravan. She had been up to the village that morning and bought huge stocks of food, even down to the local newspaper, which she said she never read herself – For a moment I felt like a king being showered with gifts by an obedient subject.

"Now, shall I cook you something before we go?" she chirped.

Having noticed the state of the cooker as I walked by with its dirty pots and pans sitting on it, all with greasy water floating in them, I thought it wouldn't be too ungracious to decline; making the excuse that we really wouldn't have enough time, so a bowl of cornflakes would be just the job."

After quickly getting through that, in case I had time to think too much about the washing-up facilities – for by now it was obvious Megan wasn't really into housework; I asked if I could use the toilet. Whereupon she opened a door; prompting a cascade of empty cardboard boxes from within to fall about the floor before us; and exclaimed with complete abandonment that, "it was in here!" Peering in, I was soon convinced that it was no longer in general use, as the place was still crammed full of boxes despite the mass exodus.

"Perhaps I had better go outside" I mumbled trying not to show my surprise; a suggestion which she readily took up.

While standing at a suitable tree, I frantically tried to sort out some of the questions which were by now tumbling into my head. Does she ever have a bath, because there doesn't appear to be one, or even a tap? Neither can there be any toilet facilities, of even the most basic kind; otherwise why am I standing here like this? So where does she go? And where is she getting her water from? Upstream from here I hope! And, what a joke – I had brought my electric shaver with me.

By now it was beginning to get dark, and as I wandered back to the caravan I wondered what she did about light. Well, I suppose we'll face that problem when we get back from the meeting later on, by which time it's going to be pot black down here, I thought.

Amongst the gloom, I made my way inside again – there was no sign of Megan, so I thought she must be changing somewhere, but quite where that would be, I couldn't make out. What I must do, I thought, as soon as we get to the Ship in Dolgellau where the AGM was to be held, is to get down to the gents as quickly as possible, and do all I have to, because there ain't going to be much chance of doing anything civilised back here. Just then, a partly obscured door at the back of the caravan opened, and a shadowy figure emerged. "We had better be off then" she exclaimed – so we did.

At the hotel, I dropped my passenger off at the door then went to park the car. As soon as I returned, I made a beeline for the gents to get freshened up.

By the time I got back, several of the society members were already waiting about in the lounge.

Throughout my life I have always known that one should never take things at face value; even so, I have had one or two nasty shocks, where things have not always seemed as they first appeared. As for women, I haven't had much experience of them either, even in my youth, having not had many girl friends, and being a bit naïve. So when I did eventually find the right one, I got on and married her. Partly because of this lack of experience I suppose; as I walked into the lounge, I wasn't as prepared as I might have been, for the sight of the sheer unbelievable re-make that could be achieved by a person.

In the gloom of the caravan I had assumed that when she emerged from the door of her room, Megan must have changed from her Wellingtons and mac; but into what I hadn't much of a clue. If anyone could have pulled off the ultimate conjuring trick, I reckon, this was it. How, I thought could anyone who lived in the abject squalor that this woman had just walked out from, perform such a magnificent piece of deceit? All credit to her, to achieve that sort of transformation without running water, or even 1/2" of clean living space takes a bit of doing. But here she was, quite remarkably and tastefully dressed in a smart knee length, close fitting black outfit, complimented with black tights and high heels to match; and carrying the whole thing off with superb ease. There wasn't a trace of dirt, dust or dog hair anywhere, and I couldn't imagine for one minute, how she could possibly have got from the caravan to the car through an inch or two of mud without some signs of it on her shoes – but there was not. – She was absolutely spotless and immaculate.

Ever since that experience, when I think the whole lot could be summed up with the sausage and skin quote; I have a quiet chuckle to myself whenever it is I see an immaculate-ly dressed woman, and wonder where she might have come from.

By the time we got back again to the caravan, after the meeting it must have been about 11pm.

"Just a minute, shan't keep you" the wizard of illusion called over her shoulder, as she hopped from the car and dis-appeared round the back of the caravan; returning a short while later dragging a small generator set, and promptly set-ting about frantically pulling on the starter cord without suc-cess. "I don't think she has ever used this thing before", I thought to myself as I gave it a quick jerk, and the lights in the caravan flickered into life; otherwise she could have got it going in a flash – which means she probably spends the evenings alone in the dark whilst Emlyn is in hospital I sup-pose. At this point I stopped being amazed at every revelation around every corner, and began to feel sorry for my hostess; that both she and Emlyn were living out their lives in a way which was so vastly different from mine.

Soon my musings were shattered by a cheerie. "I have made up a bed for you at the front of the caravan. I sleep through here," she said, opening the half-concealed door at the rear, which was the signal for another bunch of dogs to dart from nowhere, and rush in and leap onto the bed. "I'll see to the lights in about 20 minutes" she said, as she followed the dogs in, and with that, wished me good night, shutting the door behind her.

Picking my way through the clutter to the made-up bed at the front, I wondered how much sleep I was going to get that night. At the best of times I'm a pretty cold mortal, and in the depths of winter, value the luxurious warmth of an electric blanket, above the imagined ultimate luxury of a Rolls Royce: and although it was only the beginning of October, down here amongst the damp and darkness of the valley, it felt more like deepest January.

I stood for a moment looking at the bed and trying to summon up the courage to undress and get into my pyjamas. As I took them from my overnight case, my eye caught sight of the toilet bag, which contained the soap, toothpaste and toothbrush. Where was I going to use stuff such as this? Was I expected to go outside? After all, there was plenty of water lying around out there, but I soon dismissed the idea. Even if I knew where the water was coming from, I didn't fancy paddling around in all that mud just to have a wash and clean my teeth, and it struck me again, how remarkable it was that our values can change in an instant so dramatically. To think that simple everyday items, which we take so much for granted, can suddenly become so important to us. – Perhaps, I thought, I'm pampered, but then, as I drew the covers of the bed back, I began to feel strangely homesick.

As the summer suns fade and give way to the long shadows of autumn, the dews become heavier each morning and the misty rain hangs from the branches, the leaves, having lost their vibrant greens, begin to fall lifeless to the ground where they lie wet and rotting, and then it is that the dark drab smell of the fading year throughout the wood fills the air. Just as the air, which was now about me, filled with the same dark drab smell; only this time, not from the rotting leaves in the wood, but from the damp bedclothes on my bed.

Morning did eventually come, but cold and damp are not all that conducive to sleep – so it was a longish night. Although on occasions, I have in the past woken on a hot clammy night, wet with perspiration, never do I remember being woken from the wet of a damp bed. It was easy then to get up that next morning; there would be no lying about wishing for another hour left on the clock. In no time at all I was dressed and ready for breakfast. No mucking about having to shave, clean my teeth or wash and, with a quick pee against the nearest suitable tree, no feeling of guilt either, because what else could I do?

Having eaten another bowl of cereals, different ones this time from yesterday, and being careful not to give Megan the impression that I couldn't wait to get away; she helped me hitch up the trailer. I thanked her for my stay, we shook hands, I asked to be remembered to Emlyn, and hoped he would soon be out of hospital and fit again. – Although I have always had a sneaking suspicion that she wouldn't be passing that message on, for I don't reckon he ever knew I'd been there. I set off, and after climbing back out of that wet slot in the earth's crust, I made for the nearest phone box to reassure Pat that I was still alive and well. She, on the other hand was more than surprised to get a phone call from me at all, thinking that something dreadful must have befallen me: which of course it had.

Having dried out by now in the comfort of a warm car, I had plenty of time for reflection as I drove home and I found myself wondering why anyone should want to live like that, for I was convinced that even if money was that tight, there must have been another way. The one thing that wasn't lacking though, during my brief stay, was the usual unreserved welcome given me, which is always so characteristic amongst the people from that part of Wales; and I thought of all those groceries she had got in for my visit, and a feeling of guilt crept over me, that I should have ever felt in my mind more preoccupied by the surroundings, than the kindness and warmth of that welcome.

Even so, I have never before enjoyed a hot bath so much in my life, as I did the one I had when I reached home.

CHAPTER 9

Committee Meeting of The Gwartheg Hynafol Cymru
(Ancient Cattle of Wales)
At The Royal Ship

"Just Dewi and Geraint to come now, and we can get started" said John Preese. Considering there were only four of us in the room at the time, those extra two would swell the numbers enormously. Eventually Dewi arrived and sat behind me, swallowing himself amongst the rows of high backed chairs which had earlier been religiously set out by the staff of the Royal Ship at Dolgellau in readiness for our meeting.

Whether, when a room was made ready for a meeting, all the chairs must always be used and put in neat rows; or whether it was that they thought the Committee of the Ancient Cattle of Wales was a vast affair, with endless streams of very important looking people arriving, carrying brief cases bulging with documents, I have never inquired; it probably depended on what John Preese had been telling them over the years I suppose. Anyway, always it is, the room appears this way. Very formal it looks too. At the front, in the bay, with their backs to the window, sits Bruce McCay the secretary, and John Preese the chairman and treasurer. A few years ago I might have said that this was a risky place to be sitting, for until recently The Ship had seen many years of neglect, and a first floor bay window there might be a bit dodgy, but work had been done, and the painters had come and gone, so that once more confidence was restored, and trade now seemed steady.

In some ways, parts of The Ship look as if they could still be back before the war, when only the privileged few frequented such places, touring Wales by motor car, and enjoying over-night stops in rather splendid, reliable old country-town-hotels. Even now, when you walk through the front doors, over the soft noiseless carpets, the staff are still there, smartly dressed in their white blouses and black skirts, and what looks like black stockings, although I hope, judging by the lack of material in their skirts, and for the sake of decency, those stockings must now have given way to something a little more substantial.

In most places cream paint lost its appeal after the war, and people were glad to have something a little brighter, so everything got covered up with white, that is, all except The Ship, where everywhere cream paint is still in all its abundance, around the reception hall, along the corridors, up the grand flying staircase, and creeping its way, even into the bedrooms. What I like most of all though, are the starched white linen table cloths in the dining room; there are no easy clean polyurethaned wood table tops here, which, with a flick of a damp cloth, wipes off the debris from the last diners. Here the Georgian plaster wall-panelling is tastefully decorated, and there is still that feeling of good old solid elegance without seeming to be too ostentatious, and where change has been resisted for what it is, and old-fashionedness, or out-datedness, as some would call it, is still proud to be on show. Whether soft music from the speakers hidden about the place is good or bad I am not sure; that must depend on those who flick the switches I suppose. Although, one day, when I thought they could do a bit better, I tried to persuade the girl at reception to put in a tape I had brought along, to try and get just a little more culture into things, with some light piano music from a few of the better shows; she managed to side step it quite nicely, by informing me that "the machine only played CDs."

It is here at The Ship, I often wonder, if I get the chance to grow old without being taken first; will there still be anyone else left about anymore who will, with me enjoy those things, which, although appearing, perhaps a little faded at times, holds onto that charm which is from a softer, gentler past? Or whether, even this will need to change to keep the place commercially viable, and the customers still coming. In some ways these changes have already happened in part, even at The Royal Ship. The bar is noisy, and full of youngsters, the decor here has, at some time suffered badly at the hands of a Philistine pub fitting firm; and tucked away down the passages at the rear of the building, on the way to the gents, are all sorts of doors hiding away even more youngsters with even louder noise. As I scuttle past these doors to the solitude of the gents, it is here once more this year, I can just give a little sigh, and quietly smile to myself as I turn off the hot tap on the hand basin, and wait to hear the same old familiar rattle and clonk of the copper pipe as it runs back across the corner of the ceiling; the timing is exactly the same, the pitch of the rattle and the depth of the clonk are as I always remember them being when I first came to The Ship, more years ago than I care to remember: and those gentle words of the refrain from that old song which Louis Armstrong made so famous come back to me, "And I say to myself, what a wonderful world"

Where opposites exist side by side, as in The Ship, there is often a space where the two are drawn together, a place, on the one hand, which is neither new and brash and noisy, so

97

that the conversation needs to be conducted half an inch from your neighbour's ear. Or where, on the opposite hand, the soft pile of the carpets, the heavy curtains at the windows, and the expensive paper on the walls make the waitresses seem like angels, gliding silently amongst the tables, unflusteringly tending their guests, and the clink of the teaspoons have that muffled ring about them. Here, the conversation is discreet and soft, so as not to attract the attention of those around. Unless you, of course, on that particular day, have the unfortunate experience of witnessing the antics of one of those insufferable people, who thinks the whole world can't wait to hear what sort of week they've had. It is to that space, between those two opposites for which I always make. A tight little corner with only a few tables, at the back of the bar, and far enough away from the noise; where the food is cheap and good, the company gets on with itself, and doesn't intrude into anyone else's, and where I can enjoy a twice a year giant plate of burning hot stir-fry. (Chinese I'm told), and it is to this spot, when The Ancient Cattle of Wales committee meet, and when the AGM is held, do I come, before the meetings begin in the room above.

"Although Geraint hasn't arrived yet, I think we should begin", John Preese murmured in English. Now, when or who decided that all meetings should be conducted in English, I have never asked, perhaps it was, that the secretary being an Irish Scot, living in Wales, and understanding not too much Welsh was the cause, or whether it was considered more businesslike - it could be. Nevertheless, that is how it is; and the same is the way of things at the local farmers mart where the auctioneer shouts in English, at a speed so great, in an accent so strong that to the unschooled he might as well be speaking fluent Welsh. Always, I can never bid for any of the first dozen or so animals when I arrive, for fear of thinking he said something different from what he did say. Only after listening carefully to the way of his words do I have enough courage to join in.

Having attempted to start the meeting, John Preese was still unable to proceed because it meant reading the agenda, for which he would need his glasses, and with which he had come without. No sooner said, than from the depths of the chairs sprang Dewi, valiantly waving his own specs., and only too pleased, I suspect, for an excuse not to struggle with the reading of the English written agenda. Soon there was great joking and excited talk between them, followed by a triumphant roar from John Preese as he put on Dewi's glasses and finding he could now read. What was said during that brief exchange, neither I, nor the secretary, from his bemused expression, had a clue, but the Welsh flowed freely for a while, and it was only then that I realised, it is out of great consideration for the English amongst us that these people were prepared to struggle with our language during that evening.

As there were still only five of us in the room until correspondence, when Geraint finally arrived, and also hid himself amongst the chairs at a safe distance from the top table; nothing had stirred the assembly too much. At this point John Preese, who being rather restless, quickly took this opportunity, as the secretary rose to his feet, to slither out through the door.

The British Cattle Movement Service is one of the many curses of today's beef farmer. It stands for red tape, red tape, and more red tape, in the cause of re-opening an export market for beef which our own politicians had effectively closed by panicking the world over B.S.E. If anyone deserved the wrath of our Irish Scottish secretary, living in Wales, it is the BCMS, and his wrath is what they got, in an endless barrage of letters asking them why they had not included in their list of approved British Beef Cattle, all the named types covered by Gwartheg Hynafol Cymru, (The Ancient Cattle of Wales)? Needless to say; if after the expected unhelpful reply to his first enquiry he had simply sent them a photograph of himself, he would have received their full co-operation, and utmost respect from then on. To describe Bruce McCay as looking like an angry old Highland bull would enable anyone to pick him out from the largest of crowds. Despite his appearance, from under those thick bushy eyebrows peep the most mischievous twinkling eyes and it is those eyes that give him away but, because they lurk there, half hidden, the casual observer is not always able to detect this secret, and therefore never discovers his true character. For a man on the other side of seventy, the proliferation of hair is not just confined to his eyes, his head also sprouts a thick mass of wild bushy white thatch which I am sure can only be combed by borrowing the toughest of wire curry combs from his cow shed.

During his long discourse, McCay retrieved letter after letter from his battered New Zealand apple box lying on the floor beside him, which acted jointly and severally as brief case and home filing cabinet. This device sums up perfectly the basic, down to earth, no frills approach of a very clever and capable man, who despite his appearance and dress, usually by way of army surplus combat Jacket, camouflage trousers and heavy black boots, provides the Society with a wealth of information and genetic knowledge.

"No doubt, as the correspondence with the BCMS is still active and incomplete, I will be able to tell you more in five months time at the AGM., when hopefully we will have twisted their arm sufficiently to include all our typed cattle in their list", he said. In the meantime no one would be surprised to learn that the Civil Service had needed to increase their staff quite considerably to cope with the extra workload caused by a little cattle society from the depths of Wales.

Computers are something I am unfamiliar with; I suppose some of my feeling towards them is a hardened resistance within me not to fall into the trap so many seem to - of having one because it is fashionable, and then desperately searching round to give the wilful monster something to do in case he takes you over, apart from which, there are lots of things I would rather spend my money on, if I had enough to be burning a hole in my pocket that is.

I came across a chap the other day who must have spent hours on his computer printing all sorts of funny tickets for a church coach outing, when all he needed to do was to make a list of those who were coming, and tick them off as they arrived. Just like we always used to – simple!

To most on the Committee of the ACW a computer is rather like a domineering wife; useful, provided somebody else handles her. So it was, we all enthusiastically agreed years ago that the Society's herd book should be put on a computer, which would avoid the duty of having it printed each year to keep all the breeding records up to date. However, after buying something second hand and discovering a year later it was useless, (someone had seen us coming, which would not be surprising), the secretary was still scratching around trying to find a handler for the replacement - now two years on.

So the computer was next on the agenda. "Well", said McCay, sucking in as much air as he could muster, hoping for sustenance to deal with this lengthy and highly sensitive saga," "I am still trying to find an operator for this wretched thing, but we have at last made some progress, and I think that very soon, by the end of the year, possibly, we should be well on the way to getting the herd book organised onto it". There were times when our beloved secretary behaved a little like a politician, and this would be such a time; the give-away words are generally, progress: think: very soon: end of the year: possibly: and, on the way: which of course means, "Don't expect anything too soon, because it might never happen." With that up to date and informative report shuffled away until the AGM, McCay quickly sat down with a sigh of relief, keeping his gaze firmly fixed on the floor in case anyone should be brave enough to ask why the whole fiasco was taking so long anyway? Of course, he need not have worried, for no one did, as we all fully understood the frightening complexities of these wonderful electronic gadgets, and wouldn't dare venture a question, even if we could begin to form one in our minds, and then attempt to put it into words as well. So for a few

101

deathly moments the room remained hushed as if those present were respecting the secretary's difficulties, with a two
minutes silence.

The secretary, having returned to his seat; John Preese
again arrived back in the room, which by now must have been
for the third time. Naturally those of us who had noticed his
activities were beginning to be a little anxious about his intake
of fluids down in the bar prior to the meeting, although no
one, admittedly had noticed anything untoward in his behaviour to explain this, which left us with only one other thing,
and that was the weak state of his poor bladder. Fortunately,
no one need to have worried, for within a very short time, the
proceedings, to everyone's relief were interrupted again by the
real cause of his constant comings and goings. Into the room
fell a fraught! overworked little waitress, bearing half filled
cups and half filled saucers of coffee - apologising profusely
for the mess and the delay; having narrowly missed complete
disaster by managing to hang onto the tray as she tripped on
the stairs in her haste to avoid yet another confrontation with
John Preese who had obviously put the fear of God into her,
on his third attempt to get some service.

Eventually, after more discussion and complaints about the
Government, Europe, mindless armchair "countrylovers" of
all descriptions, and the endless hoards of so-called "experts",
all intent on telling us what they think we should be doing
with "their" countryside; we came to Any Other Business.

There had been a letter from a member in Scotland who
was looking for a good Belted bull, as his present one would
soon be serving his daughters, so he needed to bring in fresh
blood. The nearest known bull to Scotland which was for sale,
we were told by the secretary, was to be found near
Southampton; this of course would present the tactical problem of transporting him without incurring enormous cost; but
then the chairman, in a wise voice reserved for such occasions, reassured us that there were, as he put it, "ways and
means", and we were to leave it to him to organise. - I am told,

that in some of the off-shore islands of Scotland they do in fact swim the bulls out from the mainland tied to a rowing boat. Whether this was the sort of thing John Preese had in mind I am not sure. So with lots of funny strange thoughts swilling round in our heads, provoked by this last remark of his; the meeting was declared closed.

After a short space of quiet, as if those present in the room were expecting something else to happen; the voice of John Preese could be heard mumbling away to Dewi in the corner. Gradually, the attention of us all was drawn in that direction, and sure enough, that which we had been waiting for, was, as we had hoped; beginning to happen. "Do you know", he said, sensing he had, by now, everyone's ear. "All this red tape and officialdom is getting so bad en it"? We all knew by these few, well chosen words that he was about to embark on one of his tales, which was bound to hold us in disbelief for the remainder of the evening. So with the business firmly behind us, we all settled down for some good entertainment, and the hanging on of every word, as it fell from his mouth.

"A few weeks ago", he continued, "I brought a couple of my store cattle to the mart in the trailer as usual. As I opened the back to unload them I noticed this animal welfare woman from Welshpool hanging about: nasty piece of work she is too. Then sure enough, she began to come over towards me, trying to get a look at the inside of the trailer as she came. 'That's an 11 foot trailer you've got there, isn't it? So where is the partition?' she said; snappy with it too she was. Maybe I should have just kept quiet and agreed with everything she said, but there, standing before me was this miserable human-cow, chucking her weight about as if the Gestapo was still alive and well in Wales, so I thought I wasn't going to let her get away with that. 'Eleven feet, how do you know that? I think you had better go off and get a tape and measure it then'. I said. Of course, when she eventually got back with the tape, and measured it, the trailer was how I knew it was all the time; eleven feet. 'I'm going to have to report you for this infringement of regulations', she said. Sure enough, two weeks later, through the post, came this letter from the Animal Health at Aberystwyth, saying they were going to prosecute me for not having a partition in my trailer".

"Do you know, the next bit takes some believing" John Preese said, with his eyes narrowing, and his thin lips tightening, as if he was living the whole thing all over again. "A few weeks later, and before I was due to appear at the court, this woman was in the mart again, but this time she was bringing in some of her own stock; rams, they were, in the back of a pick-up truck: (she has this bit of a place over towards Welshpool). Anyway, as she was lifting one of them out of the back of the truck he got his foot caught in the tailboard, and was hanging there; he was too heavy for her to lift back so that he could get his foot out again, and so he was just stuck where he was. Now, a few of us were watching all this going on with a lot of interest, and so we went over to help her sort out the problem; and very grateful she was too. Of course, it has been illegal for a while now to carry stock in the back of a pick-up, I suppose for the very reason that she had got into trouble over". John Preese stopped, a glimmer of a grin began to show itself in the corner of his mouth, and his eyes glinted, half closed, as he paused, and slowly looked about his audience. We all waited in silence. If anyone could have peered into the heads of those there that day, they would, I am sure, have seen the same thing in each of them; not believing his luck, and wishing for the day when we could all have such an opportunity presented to us on a plate like this.

After he was sure that every eye in the room was on him, he continued. "The next day, I thought I had better not waste any time, so I got straight on the phone to Aberystwyth, and asked for the boss of Animal Health; the one who had written the letter to me, about going to the court later in the year. When I was put through – 'Hello Mr. Preese – you got my letter did you? You should be appearing in September.' 'Ah yes, I know all about that. That's not what I'm phoning about. Did

104

you know that I saw Miss Davies in Dolgellau Mart yesterday?' I said: and I started to tell him about what we had seen, and how we had helped her with the ram. When I had finished there was no sound from the other end of the line – not a sound – just silence. 'Mr. Lloyd, are you still there?' I called. Then a soft voice came back. – 'Yes yes. – I think I had better be writing to you, Mr. Preese.'

In the post the next day was a letter from Aberystwyth, which told me that if I took the matter in Dolgellau no further, I would not have to appear in the court". "So what did you do?" came all of our voices – hoping that he would not be seen to be doing a deal with the bureaucracy. "I just settled for that", he said. – He knowing that thus far would be far enough; and that this very valuable card was, after all, still sitting up there in his sleeve, and should help bode well for a quieter life at the Mart in the future.

"That's right, very clever", came the general murmur of approval from all about us. "Nothing like using their own stick to thrash them with is it?"

Our evening that day had been rounded off with the telling of that tale, to the great satisfaction of us all; and it sat in our minds to show us that we didn't always lose out to our masters all the time: for there were probably, out there, more of them than us now; so the bringing down of one or two of them by a well aimed shot was a good tonic to us all. So, with all that happiness ringing in our minds, we eagerly shook the hands of the others, and went off back to the isolation of the hills.

FOOTNOTE

We were at the Ship again this year. I'm sorry – the plumbing won't perform for you as it used to for me – they've altered it.

And the waitresses – those smart white blouses and black skirts have gone. They look more like mental health nurses now with their blue loose tops, yellow aprons and black trousers.

The music – that's still a problem. We've got CDs now, so I'm going to have another try next year

CHAPTER 10

George

Tan-y-Bryn (Welsh for Under-the-hill) Awel was one of our Belted Welsh cows – born and bred on the place, and daughter of Coedwr Awel, an eleven year old cow of ours, who had been born and raised in the hills around Dolgellau. Young Awel (as she was known), this year had become a bit of a mystery. Here we were in August, and she still hadn't calved, when everyone else had finished calving by the middle of June. Reassuringly the vet had done a P.D. (pregnancy diagnosis) on her back in July and confirmed that all was right inside and that she must have been late coming on bulling – but, "there definitely was a calf in there."

That Sunday morning I had checked the stock as usual, and all was well, with young Awel behaving normally, as if she wasn't expecting anything today. During that afternoon we had one of the heaviest thunderstorms I can ever remember, but it was soon over, and the sun returned to a perfect day.

Normally, if we are expecting a calving I look round the stock several times a day for telltale signs; but the vet's P.D.

107

verdict was for a calving sometime in September, so the early morning checks would be all I needed to do.

Confident that all was as it should be we visited friends in the evening, and it was only then, quite suddenly, during that visit, and for no apparent reason, a doubt began to form in my mind. As the evening wore on the doubt began to become a nagging force so great that I had become, by the time we left, desperate to get home and down the field.

By the time we had reached the house I had convinced myself the chances of Awel having calved that day were pretty high. I don't know why I felt this so strongly – I just did. Neither is it the first time this has happened. In the past, during the night I have been woken with the same overwhelming force to go out and check the cows; and it had often turned out, for good cause too.

The heavy cloud had brought the darkness early that evening, and as I walked across the field, I cast the beam of the flash light back and forth waiting for it to catch the little white lights, which would be the eyes of a cow reflecting back as she gazed at me. Sure enough, after only a few minutes, there it was, and something was with her too, for the "white lights" kept disappearing as she looked away from the torchlight to the ground near her.

As I reached the spot where the cow was, and saw, as I thought, that it was Awel, she appeared to be standing alone, but her anxious furtive staring glances alerted me, and I could just about make out a little, still black form in the bottom of the hedge. Was this a live calf, or was the cow simply standing there grieving over a dead one?

I shone the torch more closely into the hedge and saw the familiar outline of a sleeping calf, with his head tucked into his side. He had been licked clean by his mother, and was perfectly dry: a picture of peaceful contentment. She too was sharing with him that same contentment as she gently moved close to me, sniffing my hand to re-assure herself of who I was; and when satisfied, lowed softly with the approval and unmistakable pleasure of a mother, proud to show off what she had achieved, and glad of the responsive encouragement in my voice, at recognising that achievement.

For the next moment we both paused, and together looked intently at what it was that concentrated our two minds in those seconds. She, with her huge form and simple brain, governed largely by instinct and habit; and me, huddled close to, beside her with my supposedly more sophisticated mind. It was, in normal circumstances, that those two minds existed poles apart, but for this tiny space in time, they were knitted so closely together, with the exact same thoughts that blocked every other thought out. How different in reality we were, and yet, how close for those moments we had become.

Just then the calf's ear flicked and he lifted his head towards us. – But he saw nothing – for his eyes were sightless and empty – the little flat sockets lifeless.

Crouching there in the torchlight against the hedge, I think the sight before me will remain in my mind for the rest of my life. This sad little creature, his head weaving to and fro, seeking for clues as to what it was that had woken him from his sleep. The darkness of that sleep was as the darkness of that night: and it would be the same darkness that would remain always with him for the whole of life before him.

I encouraged the little form from the closeness of the hedge, which despite his blindness he had sought out as being the nearest reminder of his previous home, in the enveloping warmth and softness of his mother's womb. My greatest concern now, was that, because of his shocking disability he might never have managed to feed from his mother, and that, even though she had so obviously cared for him, as her strongest mothering instincts would have caused her to do: never would those instincts have prepared her for this ordeal. He could, in actual fact be lying here in apparent contentedness, when instead it might be complete exhaustion provoked by the ordeal of attempting to reach out for his vital first feed. To my relief, when standing him on his feet, his tummy was full, his nose and ears warm, and his dung lay where he had slept. – Instinct and smell are wonderful, aren't they?

As I examined this silent little figure standing there before me in the dim torchlight, my relief was to be overtaken yet again with disappointment.

My hand, as it travelled over his back in a gesture of comfort towards him, stopped before reaching its end. Two thirds of the way along his back, where the tail would have begun to be formed from the spine, there was – Nothing – Suddenly – Nothing – That is save a raw little end to his spine; and where the tail was to have lain along the remainder of the back, there was just a shallow channel in which nothing had formed. Not only would this little chap never have the pleasure of sight, he would also be unable to perform the most spontaneous of gestures; that of the endless lazy swatting of flies during the hot summer days.

What really was to become of this lonely little soul, shut away in all his darkness. If his markings were an indication of his form, then he would have been perfect, for his white belt, wound round his body, in complete uniformity of width, and of not too generous, or too pinched in proportions. It was, as well, pitched in exactly the right spot along his length.

As I left this unfortunate pair, after satisfying myself that there was nothing more I should do, and being content that he was in the best care, that even man with all his proud knowledge and arrogant ways could have provided, I wondered about their future together. For each, in their own way, it was bound to be a difficult journey. For me too, this was uncharted waters, never had I come across, or even heard of a blind calf before: and the questions and doubts began to well up in my mind.

Would he survive, no matter how good a mother he had? Would he cope, no matter how resourceful he might be? And even if they conquered this enormous physical handicap between them, each drawing on the limits of their own natural instincts; might there just be something else within that little body that could be malformed? Something else unknown and unseen by the three of us, and of which, not even the most gentle patient and understanding qualities of this mother would be able to wrestle with, and win through? But only time would provide that answer. Even by the morning this unknown deformity, if it were there, could have taken its toll on that new life, and had its devastating effect on his hopeful innocent mother.

Making my way back home across the dark field that night, my last thoughts were of her, with the happiness and pride of a new mother; and him, in all his contentedness of the warmth and comfort of a full belly, and the softness of his grass bed against the friendly hedge, and how I wished that it would always remain for them. For neither knew, or could even begin to comprehend that it might be any different; and I thought of the sweetness of their innocent ignorance, and of what could befall them both by morning. To me, even the thought brought concern, but the sleep, which was to escape me that night, would at least be theirs.

Morning eventually came, and it was with a certain dread that I crossed back over the field again, to where I had last seen that little couple on the previous night.

Long before reaching the spot, I could see that they were no longer there. This was encouraging, and changing direction I soon came upon them; she grazing peacefully, and he wandering about exploring this new place which was full of sounds and scents, but strangely cloaked in darkness, even so; this to him made no difference. On hearing me approaching, he stood motionless, and with his head raised to catch my scent, he looks towards me, he blinks, but nothing is looking out from those tiny empty eye sockets. Soon she is beside us, lowing and fussing her way about the two of us, pride in her voice, and I wondered then if she understood the truth of what to me was so obvious. Very often, when we are close to something, it is then that we are unable to see what can sometimes be wrong with that thing. Perhaps it is nature's way of protecting us. Mothers with newborn babies do not always notice what others see when something is not right with a baby. Or maybe, the overwhelming love of that tiny life, no matter how it looks, is to that mother the thing which outweighs all else; and for that anyway, on this day, I was glad, because that bond, which is so beautiful to see in animals, was as strong here as I have seen anywhere.

Now it was daylight, I had my first chance to examine this calf more closely, and everything I had noticed the night before was exactly how it was. But as my eyes and hands passed over him, suddenly my heart sank, for under his belly there was no penis, just the remains of the dried umbilical cord hanging and waiting to fall away, as it usually did within a day or two. It would be only a matter of time now before this poor little soul would be in tremendous agony, and we would be left with only one option, and that was to put him down.

The greatest and earliest lesson I ever learned about farming was never to be too optimistic about anything. If there was 50/50 chance of something good coming from anything, make up your mind that something bad would turn up instead. Just the same we are never completely convinced that things are always this way, and straw clutching is what we do best.

Now that I was faced with this awful dilemma, how was I to set about the mechanics of dealing with the problem? There would be no question as to who should do it; never in a thousand years could I bring myself to end the life of one of our own. We must get the vet as soon as we could, and with a gentle squeeze of his syringe this little life would be quietly taken from us. That of course then leaves us with a grieving cow, something I have always had enormous difficulty in dealing with, and which in turn, if we don't watch out, as her teats have already been opened up with the sucking calf, could end up with mastitis.

All these things were swirling round in my mind; although, as usual, underlying all this thinking and increasing depression, there still remained the ever familiar sense, that whilst there was life, there was hope. As I was pondering all these thoughts; quite suddenly, this little creature, standing beside me, tucked his back legs under his body, arched his back, and peed out of his bottom. – I stood for a moment watching in disbelief. – He's a heifer I murmured – half cross with myself for making such a stupid and basic mistake, but at the same time overjoyed that she might now, at least have a start in life, and I wouldn't have to face the wretched business of dealing with her departure.

On the second day of this little life, by the time I had come out into the field, she had already fed, and I knew, if her mother wasn't so good, that little calf would never live – She is so patient with her, as she tries to find the way to her mother's udder.

Each morning they are in a different place in the field. The calf feeds, is looking strong, and walks well. Although it is quite upsetting to see this little thing, holding her head in the air, trying to sense whether anyone is about, how lonely it must be for her, but in a way, her mother does her best to compensate with her encouraging sounds.

That evening, as I came away, I felt a strong and growing bond between us, with the question in my mind. How was I after another 2 and half years going to be able to send her off with the other fat cattle? What was I going to do, we are supposed to be in this business to earn a living – sentiments should not be a part of that; but whether they are or not, the fact remains that sentiments have an overwhelming power, which I find difficult to resist.

Almost a fortnight had gone by; and one morning I noticed, unusually, that the calf was still lying down under the lime tree, only a few yards from where she was the day before. Her mother and grandmother were both together, standing just a short distance away. I am beginning to be suspicious that all is not well. There is little activity, but at the same time, a quiet uneasiness. As I move towards the calf, she lifts her head, which I stroke, and she responds, obviously enjoying the moment. Soon we are joined by her mother uttering her, by now usual soft reassuring grunts. The grandmother too is now nearby, standing silently, watching out intently for the youngster.

By the next day I am sure this little calf cannot be getting enough milk, she is listless and only a few yards from where I left her the previous day with her mother some distance away. The chances are, if she hasn't been feeding properly she will start to become dehydrated, her nose and ears are barely warm. I decide to put her on a course of what I call the magic mixture; this is a pink powder called Energin, which balances the enzymes in the stomach, and stimulates the animal to feed. It is made up into a liquid and then fed with a tube straight into the calf's stomach if it is too poorly to drink; or; if it will drink, then fed from a bottle with a teat.

Our little calf was still well enough to drink and she knocked it back immediately (as they generally do; it's like feeding strawberries to a donkey). As soon as she finished the bottle of Energin, she went straight to her mother, and drained her out too.

Over the next few days she took the Energin and her mother's milk – the change was dramatic, but this still left the question. Why didn't Awel, her mother, have enough milk for her calf? There had never been a problem with this cow before, she always fed her calves well. So the risk was, unless I could get to the bottom of things, once I stopped dosing the calf, the chances are she would become dehydrated again.

Perhaps it was time for an experiment. Since the calf had been born we had had some heavy rain, but we had also several very dry days in between, and we were going through a dry spell at present. I fetched a bucket of water from the water trough, took it to Awel, and she immediately drank the lot with great enthusiasm – Just as I thought – she had never let the calf out of her sight, which meant she had never ventured to the water trough, and this had the effect of drying up her milk.

Sometimes, after a cow gives birth she will behave like this, but then, after a day or two, she will leave the calf and go for a drink. Awel had been managing by taking in the water off the wet grass as she ate, but that was hardly enough to feed her calf properly, especially when the weather turned dry. This all meant that she was, after all, very aware that her calf was not normal, and she would need to give that little soul all the care and attention she could muster. After a few days of carrying water to Awel; and the calf no longer needing the Energin because she was increasingly becoming more lively and alert; one day I noticed the cow at the trough, and realised that she had now gained enough confidence to leave her progeny unattended whilst she went for a drink.

As the days turned into weeks, and the weeks into months, George, as I had named him on that first night - George he was, and George she would remain - (named after Blind George, who played a harmonium at St. Ann's Well in the hills almost every day for over 50 years until the 1930s, and who my mother often told me about and remembered well on her frequent visits as a girl to my great aunt at Malvern), our George, continued to thrive, and amazingly, led an almost ordinary and natural existence amongst the other calves. She had no difficulty in finding her mother by now. Although by nature, and birth, Black and Belted Welsh cattle have on the whole remarkably good maternal instincts. This cow, even so, excelled, and was amongst the best.

As time passed, this young animal tended to grow away from me. I suppose, if I had had the time to handle her more the bond would have grown stronger. This distancing in fact was a Godsend, because always, from the earliest days of her life, I thought she would need to rely on me for her existence. How was I then, going to be able to face up to having to sell her? Fortunately she and her mother coped easily – (I should have known better) – I really do believe that animals adapt and compensate better than we humans. I once knew of a little dog who had been run over and became paralysed in both his back legs. His owners made a little two-wheeled trolley, which they strapped him to, resting useless limbs on it. This little device acted as his back legs, and to see him dart about as if he had been born with it was amazing, and a great tonic.

Even so, if anyone had asked me, which of the two handicaps would cause the most problems in a calf – being blind or being tail-less – I should have said being blind. In fact it was the other. On reflection though, and on experiencing both, an animal can adjust to blindness; it can learn to feed and to smell its way about, although it does need to take a great deal of care when running as it needs more distance to sense when an object is standing in its way. But to have no tail, there is nothing it can do to swat and drive away the flies. Winter is not a problem, but summer is a completely different kettle of fish.

Flies can always cause problems in stock, especially sheep – Cattle are troubled, but not to the same extent. They can become restless, and even lose weight if severely pestered. The most serious effects in cattle is an eye infection known as New Forest disease; which if not treated with creams or by injecting the lower lid of the infected eye, will result in blindness. Creams are cheaper, but need to be used each day for a week or more, so that the animal will have to be brought in, which unless they are milking cows is not always possible. I go for the easy option – the one off – Get the beast in once, get the vet, (grin and bear the bill), and if you have caught the problem in time, within a few days the weeping will stop, the eye will begin to open, the ulcer on the eye will start to shrink, and within a week or two, the beast will be back to normal.

Having said that, to inject the lower eyelid in a cow does sound a bit daunting. The secret, as always is, not to upset the animal; keep yourself calm and quiet; and that will generally be passed on to the beast. Crush them up well, and halter its head securely. The vet, if he hasn't been drinking recently, will have a steady enough hand to slip the syringe needle into the drawn-down skin of the lower part of the eye; and if everyone

116

is gentle, with a good bedside manner, then the patient will co-operate and seemingly be glad of the treatment, even if he is a bull.

Knowing the wretched ways of flies, I made a point of, each day looking, as I thought, closely, at the rear end of George for the tell-tale signs of fly eggs.

One day she appeared to be rather wet on her rear thigh. Sure enough, despite treating the tail area with fly repellent, the flies had got at her without me noticing; and not only had they managed to lay their eggs, the eggs by now were a mass of wriggling fat white grubs working away beneath her coat.

I dashed back to the house, and returned armed with a bottle of pour on fly repellent, and an aerosol of fly killer. Whilst she stood, I went about attacking her back end, and within seconds hoards of nasty little parasites surfaced and started falling to the ground like miniature parachutists, spewing from an aircraft; and the more that fell from her, the more there were to replace them, cascading to the ground in their waves, and in a never ending mass. The whole of her rear thigh appeared to be heaving with the squirming maggots, and despite all this stampeding activity by me and them, dear George remained still and calm, apparently unaware that she was in the early stages of being eaten alive. For upon closer examination, sure enough, the skin beneath her hair had become red raw, and the moisture on the coat, which had first alerted me was the beginning of decomposition of her flesh.

From then on I watched her like a hawk, carefully treating her with pour-on fly repellent and fly killer; and within a few days the wound dried up, and began to heal. During the whole of this time, poor little George never appeared to notice anything amiss. She just carried on growing and adjusting to being in the world.

Having got her underway, and in a thriving condition over the following months, I began to wonder how other people had managed blind calves. No doubt there must have been some about somewhere. Sure enough, I soon heard of a blind cow down on a dairy farm in Berkeley, not far from us. She had been reared as a youngster, and put in calf when old enough, and then used to suckle several calves, including her own. No doubt they hadn't the heart to put her down when they first discovered her condition, as she would have probably found it near impossible to integrate into a milking herd, with all the problems of large numbers of other beasts, and having to cope with going through a milking parlour twice a day. So her job in life was to look after and rear a few calves every year, which she apparently did very well.

Almost a year had gone by since the birth of our unfortunate little calf. She wintered well, very soon finding her way into the shed for feeding, which she shared in the small paddock up the lane, with a heifer from the same batch of calves; and who she appeared to have paired up with. Her growth wasn't too bad, but she would probably take longer to reach maturity than the others; so if everything went to plan, she would need to be sold in about 18 months time. This in itself, because of her blindness, I was beginning to think, might be a problem.

Bearing in mind the bureaucratic meddling that office hatched, reared and bound, morons in Whitehall practised, I thought it might be prudent to make a few inquiries – and sure enough: - Legislation states that "a blind animal may not be transported for sale or slaughter" So why? – Is it going to throw a fit? Is it going to fall over, and injure or kill itself? Will it want to see where it is going?

Endless possible reasons raced through my head, but I could never reach a good answer for not being able to transport a blind animal.

The problem we have out here is that those in the corridors of power have never been out here to see for themselves. It could never dawn on them that an animal is easily restrained and prevented from falling about by suitably arranged partitions in a vehicle. They never consult with grassroots. They think all the correct answers are given them by their own type:

the over qualified paper experts who gaze all day long into computer screens for their answers: and are convinced of their unquestionable knowledge and importance.

Anyway, what do we know about it? And why should they even begin to think of the difficulties which just about everything they expect us to do, will cause? So what was I to do when the time had arrived for George to go? Well, in their wisdom, the "experts" had condescended to say that if an animal was slaughtered on the farm, and provided it could be transported to the abattoir within one hour that would be acceptable. It so happened, thanks to E.U. legislation, which had pushed all the small local abattoirs out of business; the one we used was about, at the best time, one hour and ten minutes away. I suppose, if I arrived at one minute after the hour, the beast would be condemned and incinerated, and I would get half the value.

Like so many things in farming these days one develops an attitude of – Shove it to the back of your mind: and either, eventually you will find a way round the problem; they will change the rules in your favour, or more likely, out of your favour. In which case, no matter what you try to do legally, you won't have a snowball's in hell chance of winning. So you'll probably end up by doing something illegal to try to save the day; and that is where the problem rested. Those stupid sods in Westminster and Whitehall, thank goodness have never heard the saying: "there's more than one way to skin a cat." They are turning the British countryside into a first class training ground for bureaucratic terrorists, and I do believe many farmers are actually beginning to enjoy the challenge – The challenge of outwitting the stupidity of bad law and red tape.

Nevertheless, and despite the problems posed by the "parasitic service", George still needed to be cared for, and carefully watched.

The flies, during the summer months were constantly waiting their chance to have a go at her rear, and despite my vigilance, one morning, sure enough, they had got through my defences. This in turn provided a field day for a bunch of marauding magpies, who had been squawking around the place ever since they had flown the local nests. Ten of the blighters had decided to visit the paddock where George and her companion were. Several of them had stormed poor old George and started performing excited acrobatics on her back, where the fly blows had been busy turning into nasty little grubs. Of course, not content with fly flesh, they set their wicked sights on hers, systematically pecking away at it; and although by now they had drawn blood, George appeared to be completely unaware of the feasting attackers, and continued grazing quite contentedly. Even so, those vicious intruders looked as if they could soon do considerable damage, so George was hurriedly rushed off into the shed, where I would need to consider my next line of defence against this new enemy.

Magpies by nature are inquisitive birds, and appear always to be looking for new ways of causing trouble for us; they especially seem to enjoy something different; new technology is a favourite.

We always run a bull here with our cows because it's easier and more accurate than A.I. An old friend of mine prefers A.I., I suppose because he has problems keeping his cows from breaking out most of the time, so he would never be able to keep a bull on the right side of a fence.

A.I. is OK if you're bringing the cows in twice a day for milking, but with suckler cows, which are used solely to produce and rear a calf, (so they hardly ever come in from the fields) the chances of spotting a bulling animal are often quite difficult and time consuming. You will find that everyone is quiet, and behaving normally whilst you are there watching them, but as soon as you turn your back and walk out of the field, suddenly someone will come on bulling, and the whole lot will be riding around on each other like some sort of rodeo, and by the time you're back again the next day the chances are it's all over, and she's gone off bulling and you've missed your chance.

This, of course, is the biggest snag with A.I. and suckler cows. Just the same, one day my friend Sydney reckoned he had cracked it. He had heard of this wonderful new idea which told you when any of your cows was about to come on bulling. All you had to do was send off your money, and they would return as many little self adhesive red lights as you had cows; and then you just slapped each light on the back end of each cow, just in front of the tail head; and waited for the heated cow to light up the bulb.

The following morning, after sticking all the light bulbs on everyone the previous evening, Sydney went out to see if any were lit, he would then be able to bring the lit cow in, and have her waiting for the A.I. man to arrive, and the job would be done. No more missed bulling from now on. It would be a first class calving index, (technical terminology for getting all your cows calving about the same time).

Whether they had all been sitting around in the trees watching him putting on the shiny red lights that evening (he was convinced they must have been): because by the time he got out there the following morning, everyone of those bulbs had been pecked to bits by the Magpies.

So how do you outwit these clever little beggars, who have just started ripping my calf apart? Go back to basics I suppose. Something nice and old-fashioned. Something simple, nothing technical, which these black and white youngsters could easily suss out. I reckoned Stockholm Tar was about as basic as you could get; a good clean smell, sticky and thick.

After whacking large dollops round the end of George's back where the tail should have started; off she went, and so did the magpies, never to be seen pestering her again.

That was July; by September things were beginning to go wrong for George. She was eating all right and behaving normally, but she was scouring (diarrhoea); and it kept on. Blood tests, theories – all explored and discounted. She did, after all, look as if she had some other problem which was beginning to rear its ugly head as she grew older.

After a couple of weeks, no one could come up with any more answers. Except, as a last resort, a young vet, who had recently joined the practice, suggested we should take her down to the Bristol University Vet School at Langford in north Somerset. They would keep her free of charge, and try some further tests, provided we paid for the drugs. So we did – I took her down in the trailer, (you can apparently do this with a blind animal, if she is going for treatment – Can you believe!)

Seeing her settled in, I came away – and that was the last I ever saw of poor little George. A fortnight later, we had a phone call from Langford to say that they really could not get to the bottom of her trouble. They assumed that, like her blindness and lack of that tail, there must have been some other genetic problem, and so – Could they have our permission to put her down?

If a chap is a bit philosophical he might say – Well it was nice having her around, she did teach us a lot: and we had to rise to the challenge which came with her – and I reckon we did – and so did she – and her mother. But even so, despite doing everything we could – we lost. And now we can only console ourselves that, despite those disabilities, she really did have a good life. – For she, of course, never did realise that there was any other sort.

Thank you, George

CHAPTER 11

Foot and Mouth

As I begin this chapter on the 13th March 2001, we are in the 4th week of what will turn out to be the worst outbreak of foot and mouth disease this country has ever experienced.

The uncertainty of our present state is emotionally draining, it is difficult to really put your mind to anything, and yet to go out into the fields, and onto the hill amongst the stock is even worse: the loneliness is quite often a hard problem to cope with. Everywhere, wherever you look is a reminder of the unseen threat, which surrounds us.

Just recently, our nearest and first outbreak in Gloucestershire was 10 miles north west of here across the other side of the Severn, in the village of Blakeney. The following day that ten miles became eight, and on a farm this side of the river, and directly to the east of the first, at Frampton on Severn. There was a brisk westerly wind, which was responsible for the second outbreak. The three, damp miles across the water between the two places formed an ideal passage for the spores, as they tossed and blew their careless way towards their next unsuspecting victims.

123

Whether they be sheep, cattle or pigs, we may be sure they are so happily and innocently unsuspecting. Not for them the sleepless nights, and the constant bearing down with heavy thoughts that fill the minds of us who are their hapless keepers and guardians.

Every morning, as we each set forth, wherever it is we farm, in what we have always held in high regard, as this green and pleasant land, on our daily rounds to feed and to check our charges; and it is, when we arrive, whether it be to the byre, the pasture, the hill, or the moor: they will be waiting patiently, with the only thoughts in their minds, which is for the contentment of the filling of their bellies. They do not possess the keenness of mind, or the sharpness of eye that detects the fear and sadness in their master's ways, as his friend and helper does, and has been aware of for many days now: for a collie's instincts are always bright and alert, and he shows it in his drawing closer to you; his constant watching with his inquisitive eyes of the expressions in your face, which he hopes will give him a clue as to why it is you feel the way you do. In all this loneliness out on the hill, the little life that walks beside you, or races ahead on a fresh scent, but is soon back again, with his reassuring grin and happy smile, is the thing which still gives you the joy, that one day, when all this is over and put behind us, whether we be wretchedly caught up in it or not, makes us realise that the world in which we live is still a beautiful place, and that sorrow and fear can be overcome if we try not to dwell on it too closely, but instead, to look forward and find another way to fill our minds and occupy our hands.

To the rooks and jackdaws foraging for food on the plough-ground in the next field, life on the hill still has the same feel and look that it always had.

March is not untypical; same dull wet days with wind, followed in seconds, it seems, by a bright sunlit sky, which looks as if it is trying to chase the reluctant winter away over the distant hills: as at the same time it struggles to entice the spring from its sleep, to bring with it the warmth and gentleness, that settles on the deep wide backs of the cudding cows as they patiently wait near the round hay-feeder for their morning feed.

There is no hurry for them now to jostle and hustle each other for their proper positions round the feeder, which the older animals had selected for themselves at the beginning of the winter, leaving the remaining spaces for the younger ones amongst them to fill. For the slowness of their interest is always a good sign that the spring grass is beginning to come, even though there seems to us very little sign of it yet.

If we, like the rooks and the jackdaws over the hedge, led a life of naïve simplicity, away from the chatter and sensationalism of the modern human world, where the breeze beneath our wings at the edge of the hill would give us our thrills as we dipped and turned to catch the next lift, or the spring in the fields with its abundance of new food, would provide us with the contentment which satisfies our hunger - then to us too, the hill would seem unchanged. But through our eyes, because our minds so much colour how we see things, and any contentment and happiness is overwhelmed by the sadness of our thoughts; then the hill will, for us, have been changed.

As the first flaps of hay are tossed into the feeder, and the beasts' enormous furry black heads reach down into it, emerging again with huge amounts of sweet smelling fodder hanging from their mouths, which they quickly engulf like endless conveyor belts – their heads held high, and eyes half closed in the enjoyment of the moment. No longer do I share the pleasure of that sight, for now my eyes are desperately searching, hoping, hoping, that I will not see the tell tale blisters on the inside of those generous mouths, which for me will most certainly change my life – and end theirs.

When I eventually draw away from that tight circle of cattle in all their contentment, and make my way with our Bryn across the top of the hill; my boots, and his little white feet still wet from the disinfectant, I look down over the slopes onto the still uneaten rough tor grass beneath us. By the time we need to move the cows down below, at the beginning of April for calving, they will have finally eaten the last of this off, and the whole hill will be transformed from its brown untidy winter appearance, to the smoothness of the soft pale greens of early spring – Or will it? Will they still be here, making their mark on the landscape? Will we again, this spring have the joy and thrill of seeing their dense black forms grazing over the emerald green flush of the new grass in the pasture below, as the setting sun leaves another day, and its last brilliance fills the hillside?

It is only now, in my thoughts, that sadness begins to turn to anger – anger at the crass incompetence and arrogance of this government which will not listen, and will not learn from those who have gone before them. Why is it their stiff necks will not let them see that they are still wet behind the ears, and have not been here before, and do not always know best, and the sickening grin of spin will not make everything all right? For those who are fooled by the shallow surfaceness of the shirt-sleeved act, and the pretence to sorrow and concern, should come out here and see for themselves, the hollowness and rank stupidity of those who are grossly out of touch with the reality of our countryside.

If this concern is real, why does it take two or three days to slaughter animals that are known to be infected? Animals that are left grazing in the fields while the neighbouring farmers look on in disbelief. Why is it, when they are eventually killed, they are not immediately buried in quick lime on the spot? Why is it their corpses are then again left for days, spewing out more infection before the slow, horrific task of burning them can begin?

The answer to all those questions is simple; it is one word – Bureaucracy. – Bureau-crazy has to check the vets initial diagnosis – (two or three days), so valuable time is lost here. Bureau-crazy dictates that livestock must not be buried, because some poncy little twerp in Brussels decreed one day that watercourses might become contaminated if farm animals were buried. That has most probably never been proved, but it just seemed a good idea at the time. This sort of nonsense can cause a delay of up to almost a week, but here we have a situation, which has all the hallmarks of fast turning into a national disaster, and needs to be addressed with urgent drastic action. So why aren't we learning from the 1967/68 outbreak, and getting to grips with it, instead of just pretending we are? Forget bureaucracy, forget Brussels. Let them do their worst, because if someone doesn't act responsibly, and take this seriously, as a stock farmer I won't want to face a future after all this is over, where we continue to suffer under a government which lit the fuse in the first place.

Let us make no mistake about that. They, and they alone, were responsible for allowing foot and mouth infected meat to come into this country from countries where the disease is endemic: and then, having allowed that, have, by their mishandling and negligence fanned the flames of disaster into a raging inferno at the government altar of bureaucratic incompetence, and onto which the farmers of this country are now expected to place their sacrificial lambs.

Thousands and thousands of sheep, cattle and pigs are being destroyed because successive British governments have seen fit to allow meat from dodgy countries through our ports, to provide us with cheap food. – Cheap food? By the time all this is over it will have cost the British taxpayers billions of pounds, and the British farmers unimaginable grief and anxiety. There seems nothing cheap about that.

What man in his right mind would fill his house with fine furniture, and then not bother to keep the roof watertight. For that is what is happening here. We have some of the best breeding stock in the world, and yet we are constantly exposed to the rubbish from countries, who it seems couldn't care less about welfare or disease.

We are told the outbreak started in a herd of pigs in

127

Northumbria, which infected some of the local sheep flocks up there. Before anyone was aware of it, these sheep had been sent to two local markets, some sold-on to many other local farms, and others transported the length of the west side of the country, down to Devon, where another rash of outbreaks has taken place. All along the route, and through a variety of markets the disease has spread, backwards and forwards, depending on how the sheep from other markets had been scattered across the local farms.

Our problems in Gloucestershire were caused by sheep from Welshpool finding their way to Hereford and Ross on Wye markets, and then onto the farms in the Forest of Dean, and then inevitably across the Severn to our side.

Within days, outbreaks in sheep were occurring all over the Forest, and the Commoners flocks were now under threat in the whole area.

Suddenly, during a space of five days a herd of dairy cattle at Berkeley was infected, bringing the 8-mile distance from us, down to 5 miles.

After another five days a flock of sheep at Berkeley was lost: then two days later 700 cattle on another dairy farm within 3/4 mile of the first. The same day brought their neighbours dairy farm down and then a 5th, all in a southerly direction from the first.

In our local press appeared these poignant words, written by the sister of two brothers farming at Berkeley:

"There they stand, black and white coats clean and shining, their soft brown eyes blinking in the morning watery sun, and their breath rising in the morning air. Milking seems a little late this morning, and one or two of the more determined of them are already shifting for position to try to get into the parlour and at extra food ration first.

How are they to know that within a few hours they will all be dead, part of the cull to try to stop the dreaded foot and mouth? They have fulfilled their part of the bargain of life by continuing to pump out the milk supply that we all take for granted. They have produced their calves and have never complained. Admittedly they have taken the care they have received for granted, but is that a crime?

Each of them has been an individual to the man who has brought them into the world and tended them through their lives. They have different quirks, some must always be first, some prefer to wait, some like a particular stall, some can't wait for winter housing to be over and to get back to the lush grass pastures that are a feature of the Vale of Berkeley. What about the blind nurse cow that can hear an apple drop from a tree from the far end of the field? She won't be hearing the rattle of the farmer's bucket. She won't be able to nuzzle at pockets for cow-cake in future. Yes, she has not been a real commercial proposition for years, but she is still there. What about the farmer who has milked twice a day since he was about eighteen years of age? Who has attended the births of the calves, and hardened his heart when they left the farm for the last time at the end of their usefulness as a herd member? What will he do in the mornings now? Admittedly, as with all jobs there are times when he has wondered why he was doing it, but to him it is a way of life. Bills had to be paid, and a sense of reality had to be maintained, but that did not prevent him from caring.

How will you feel when the fields of the Vale are denuded of animals? And this is all because of a few greedy people who saw an opportunity to flout the law and make a quick buck. Maybe it is also due to the politicians who are not prepared to spend OUR money to make sure that imports into this country are what they are said to be.

Farming has been suffering for many years, but because of the tenacity and dedication of the men who tend the fields, it is still there when many other industries have gone to the wall. Farmers have to make money to pay their way, and we can criticise the few who have exploited the system, but this does not take into account the hundreds who have doggedly soldiered on and tended and cared for their animals.

When I go home tonight we will still have the horses, cats and dogs; but our lives will be that much less because of what mankind has managed to do to the cows, sheep and pigs. Many tears will be shed behind closed doors for the lives that have gone. Farmers, however, are realists and fighters. They will pick themselves backup, and hopefully will get back into the lives they know. Hopefully they can use this catastrophe to rethink many of the things that they do not like about farming. Hopefully too, the public who have been so supportive and considerate during this terrible time will help support the future development of the countryside. I am optimistic enough to think they will."

Christine Fulton
Ham, Berkeley, Glos.

During the last couple of weeks we have been shivering with a cold damp northeasterly wind, and it was now reaping its toll. The only crumb of comfort we are able to draw from this was that all the places affected are directly west from us, so that although the devastation is enormous, the disease has not drawn any closer.

Whether there is any foundation in the M.A.F.F. theory that roads provide a "fire break" I am not sure. But on this occasion they certainly did not, for within a space of a further 2 days, and only 3 miles from us, foot and mouth had crossed 2 roads, and settled nicely in a small flock of sheep, and neither had it been wind-borne, because of the present direction of the wind.

The cause, was the poor unsuspecting relief milker on one of the local farms, who had taken it home to her flock of sheep, while the disease had been unnoticed and quietly incubating in the cows she was milking.

This is now the 6th week of the initial outbreak. During this time the government has seen at last, that despite repeatedly saying the disease was under control (a sentiment which no one else with any common sense could possibly endorse): they have at last called in the army to organise logistics, of what, by now has become an enormous task. We have seen the number of confirmed cases, (that is infected farms, not stock numbers) rise from 20 on Friday 9th March to 246 by Thursday 15th March, and then onto 693 farms by Tuesday 27th March.

It was about a fortnight ago when I remember a particularly bad couple of days for us here. We had seen pictures on TV, of sheep in the Forest of Dean, happily grazing, and pumping out virus having been diagnosed as having foot and mouth 3 days earlier, whilst MAFF vets were patiently waiting for lab reports to confirm that fact before slaughtering them. If this sort of crass stupidity were to continue, the disease will run rampant over the whole country, and no longer would there be any hope for livestock farmers anywhere. The following day was a nightmare, nowhere could I get the information as to what was happening. The opposition in the House of Commons, and ordinary farmers were screaming that more should be done more quickly – Diagnosis to slaughter must be achieved within 24 hours, as emphasised in the 1969 report following the 1967 outbreak, and the army should be brought in immediately from the start to run the job, something which was in the report of that time too.

One of the many worrying aspects to emerge from this catastrophe was that nowhere could the voice of the N.F.U. be heard. It appeared that they didn't want to be seen to be criticising the government. So who pays their salaries I wonder – the government, or the farmers?

Much of the following day was spent on the telephone getting nowhere, and getting no answers, despite shouting at endless unresponsive civil servants. Unfortunately for Pat, the shouting didn't stop when I came off the phone either – Gosh, she's a brick – Can't imagine what I would do without her.

It is now 25th Feb 2002. One year and 6 days after foot and mouth disease was first confirmed in our country. Even though we haven't had a case since Sept 2001, I have only just had the will to pick up my pen and write again.

By the beginning of April 2001 the disease had struck a farm 2 miles from here as the crow flies. We were issued with a "Form D", which meant that nothing could be moved on or off the premises, and we couldn't come into contact with anything or anyone without disinfecting ourselves first. – How long before it was our turn? During this time the press was full of stories of government incompetence – animals stranded in fields with no food, overgrazed grassland where there was nothing but mud. – Lambs born in the most appalling conditions, and mostly unable to survive. Slaughtered stock left in stinking plies for weeks, just a few feet from farm houses, before being disposed of, either on enormous pyres, or transported miles to incinerators.

Down at Berkeley (6 miles from us), several attempts were made to build and light a huge pyre of rotting corpses using railway sleepers in a field, which had become a bog with all the wet weather. In the end the task had to be abandoned because the whole structure was sinking, and had become impossible to light. At one stage there was talk of moving all the carcasses onto the bypass and burning them on the road, this was aborted in favour of hauling everything 4 miles onto higher drier ground where they had more success with the fire. Even so, the heavily laden lorries, because of the steepness of the lane leading to the site were unable to grip the road surface, (Remember what they were laden with, and by now, the condition which those loads must have been in). Every available heavy tractor in the area was pressed into the service to help drag the lorries to the top.

Although of course we didn't go near the place, or even ventured off our own for some time, for there was always the fear of coming into contact with someone who had been near an infected farm, the sights on these farms would never be forgotten by those who were there. Out of the 18 farms on the Berkeley Estate 9 were either infected or taken out in the cull.

By now the disease had reached out of the Vale and was approaching our escarpment. The nearest farm to us in a westerly direction was just 1/2 mile over the hill; the news arrived with them that they would have to go in a cull. If disease was found there, then it would be our turn next.

Here is an extract from a letter we received from those neighbours describing how they felt:

"Dear Mr & Mrs Forster,

20/05/2001

Foot and Mouth disease has been a dreadful problem for the country. Devastation in Cumbria, and suddenly on our doorstep in Gloucestershire. A farm at Wick went, putting us on restrictions, my voice had disappeared through a flu type bug, there was suddenly so many telephone calls, a vet was to inspect the flock in the next 3 or 4 days, the day she arrived Gordon walked the farm with her, they had looked OK but now Fortunes Farm had gone down, putting Walter Eley in line for a cull of his animals, a few were found infected, this put us in for the cull. The telephone call came in the evening to have the flock gathered in for the next morning. Yes, after the needless walk round the farm.

Thursday April 5th. It was the most horrendous time. Alan, Gordon and the sheepdog rounded up the ewes with their lambs; lambing had nearly finished. Gordon came in, as it seemed the farm had been taken over by Aliens, all these people in either white protective suits or the yellow rain wear. Nature is so strong, disease, and now the torrential rain.

The valuer and ministry vet were to arrive at 12 noon,

followed by slaughterer, and the army at 1pm; a group of disinfectors, and members of MAFF. To drown unwanted sounds the clothes washer and dishwasher made their noise with radio spinning out music or presenters and journalists tales.

Everything was watched over by the vet who, after the slaughterer, then had to inspect every animal's mouth. It was 9pm, a call was made to head office in London, half an hour to wait; were we to be classed infected? The result to be known in the morning, 3 sheep were under question.

Next morning the army arrive, it seemed the carcasses were to be burnt, not buried as first intended, so for a short while we took it we were infected, but calls to the ministry found we had been deemed dangerous contact. So our neighbours sheep and cattle were to escape cull. It was Saturday at 1pm, the army moved the carcasses, the sounds of washing machines blotted out the noise, this time of reversing sounds as the carcasses were to be loaded into the coffin lorry, there was so much work, the army were the people to be there: (if only they had been called in earlier, they may have prevented such a spread). The soldier on duty at the farm was kind and understanding, he had known little of farming before.

We felt completely shell shocked and worn out, but Gordon has braved the storm, the first time in his life without animals. (Yes, our animals bred for the food chain, but they do not all go suddenly at once, and lambs, no chance of a life to frolic and race; you have to have a love and caring for animals, and you have to steel yourself when they go). As it happened, the next morning one of the usual forms arrived. What animals did we have?... We do have one cat, and 2 spaniels, and one collie, who is rather lost, it must have been a terrible time for the dogs; the cat appeared to have an idea of what was happening, and had a different routine for a few days. Although so many things I could do, it has been only the garden I could get lost in, so hope the results of that will show.

After two weeks confined to the farm, we now have liberty around the house, and house entrance yard. Before I was told to obtain a licence if I needed a doctor! But could run if there was an emergency.

It is now a month on ... the voice has returned we are on the up. But when do we have control of our farm? Who really had foot and mouth? When will we get money for our animals they took and slaughtered? We are in limbo as the great "clean up" goes on.

It is a big thanks for all the messages of sympathy by cards or phone; and gifts sent: the lovely pink roses I am still at a loss as to whom to thank. You all helped us so much: calls from people affected by the disease back in 1967.

Your card and thoughts were much appreciated. It will be good when the cleaners have left and we can return to some form of normality. Gordon hopes to have a few sheep in the autumn.

It has been hard coming to terms with what has, and is happening, and will we ever know the answers to so many questions?

So many have been affected in different ways and degrees.

We hope things go well with you
Sincerely, Rosamond &Gordon (Smith)

Mornings on the hill were depressing with the constant fear that the invisible enemy was all about us. Always before, I had enjoyed watching the seagulls soaring above; swooping and crying, or pecking for insects on the cattle-poached ground. But now, instead of being harmless and welcome guests up from the Severn, they had suddenly become the enemy. What was it, perhaps, they were carrying on those feet, or harbouring in their beaks. What use was it chasing them off, they would only rise on the wind, laughing and singing as they went, to return moments later and continue. So I resisted this futile act to rid myself of them, and looked the other way.

A day or two after the nearest outbreak, with the wind in the west, as it mostly is. On the air came the stench of burning flesh. Was it true, as some had claimed that this was one of the ways the disease spread? So for us, how long now?

When a man well passes middle age, the way he looks at life, and the way he plans his life, (as much as he is able to do, that is) changes. Such a time had reached us where we needed to stop and to make up our minds what we were to do with the rest of our working lives, when, (not if), this wretched thing visited us.

It was pointless just waiting about, ringing our hands and making ourselves more and more miserable wondering how we would cope with having our stock slaughtered before our eyes, and then set fire to in front of the house; for that, we felt sure, was where it would happen, because that was the only flat land on the place. We needed to look beyond that time – to take a long view of where we went from here, because if we didn't, depression would soon overwhelm us, and drag us so low that we might never recover.

It is, in time of crisis, that people turn to God for help. The churches, during the war were filled with despairing folk, not knowing where to go for help other than their creator. After those dreadful years, I fear many of those desperate people drifted away – God must have felt very let down.

Perhaps, even when a man does not just reach out to God in times of trouble, and then conveniently forgets him at other times, but is consistent in his faith, it can still take a heavy crisis to really bring him to his knees and humble him. But when that happens, God can cause a wonderful enlightenment for that person's mind; and so it was for us.

Our prayers became more earnest for some sort of help in all this; and gradually the path we needed to take began to unfold in our minds. Instead of dwelling on the details of when the disease struck, we began to think of the time beyond that. – What we should do when all this was behind us. Whether to re-stock and try again, or to just call it a day and walk away from everything.

It must have taken us just a few seconds to reach a decision. That decision was to simply walk away from it. After all, what was the point of constantly being dictated to by politicians and civil servants using the subsidy system to manipulate how we were to run our place, and to be more and more over-burdened by bureaucracy and legislation which was mostly based on the whims of headless morons in Brussels.

Once decided, we both felt great relief: so that, come what may, we reckoned now, we would stand a much better chance of coping.

Whether the government was beginning to take things seriously and move a lot quicker than they had before; or maybe we just had a good team working round here; but to everyone's disbelief, quite suddenly the disease seemed to have stopped in its tracks. This didn't of course mean that we could forget it, but as the days and weeks wore by, and no new outbreaks were confirmed, we hoped we had seen the worst in Gloucestershire anyway.

At this point, every week for 5 weeks we were visited by a Ministry vet, who walked the hill with me to inspect the cattle. – He needn't have worried, for all the inspections were carried out thoroughly by me each morning before he arrived. Cattle are easy to spot – lameness on all four feet, and blisters round the mouth. Sheep are very tricky, lameness could mean any number of things, and so could legions in the mouth. So it was, at the end of this terrible time which had lasted for 8 months, and no new cases were coming through at all, sheep everywhere had to be blood-tested before they were considered to be clear.

But the bungling by government and ministry did not stop there. No one was allowed to move anything, which meant that farms were becoming overcrowded as more young stock were being born, without the older animals being sold off, as would normally have happened.

Another of our neighbours was completely beside himself; he was unable to buy in feed for all those extra animals. Throughout the early days of the foot and mouth, which was still the winter months, some of his cattle had grown so weak from hunger that they were unable to cope with the muddy wet conditions created by the overcrowding, and they just fell dead in the mud from exhaustion. Attempting to drag the bodies out and dispose of them, knowing that tomorrow there would probably be more, and all the time realising that red tape was preventing him from getting help, it almost destroyed him too. The heavy hand of misguided and ignorant officials rendered even the RSPCA powerless, when he called on them for help.

It is no surprise that this government is doing all it can to prevent a public inquiry into the foot and mouth crisis, but make no mistake, the arrogance of these urban pratts, who seem to pride themselves of their infallibility, will be brought heavily into question, and there will be a full public inquiry, despite their protestations: and many, many of them will be found very severely wanting.

Enough of this, it makes me so depressed, even now, long after these terrible events have passed. To think that this could have happened in a so-called civilised country – I am ashamed to be part of a nation to which that sort of person in high office belongs. I only hope that this time lessons will have been learnt, but not ignored; although I fear that is not the case, for even now illegally imported meat, and meat from countries where foot and mouth is endemic is still flooding into our country.

As the sun slowly rises over a new day, so does the gentle realisation that you have been spared a terrible thing.

There is no great celebration – for what is there to celebrate?

Is it the death of countless victims caught up in a human quagmire of politics and economics?

Or the sadness and anguish of those who have cared for them, but have lost them just the same?

No – there is no cause for celebration, even though you have not borne that same heavy price.

Just the gentle realisation and grateful heart, that you have been spared.

FOOTNOTE TO A SAD CHAPTER

Despite the loud and continuous chorus of voices from everywhere, and everyone calling for a public inquiry into this unbelievably catastrophic saga, our government resisted.

This leaves us with only one conclusion, and that is, they knew all the time how badly they had let down the farmers and livestock of their country.

They refused to face the music when the time came.

They needn't have worried – We made up our minds long ago about their moral fibre: and nothing they do can hide that.

CHAPTER 12

"You Need Us"

"If you can't make a living out of farming, diversify, convert some redundant buildings to holiday cottages; open a farm shop, or do B&B – the opportunities are endless."

So say our unpractised-with-life, wet behind the ears, schoolboy politicians. We'll help you – we'll pinch some subsidy from the already hard pressed others of you, spend it on talk shops, seminars, consultants experts and dolly birds with clip boards, and then pass what's left onto you. That is, of course, if there is any left.

Oh, by the way, there will be plenty of hoops for you to jump through before you can get a penny, so we want you to tick boxes, get a business plan; which means you will of course need to attend talk shops, seminars, and employ consultants, experts and dolly birds with clip boards. And then, there definitely won't be any money left after that, so if you are still stupid, or desperate enough to want to continue down this road, go along and see your bank manager, (if you have one anymore, that is), and see if he is stupid enough to lend you the money. If he is, he will then ask you for another business plan, by which time you will have spent so much time attending talk shops, employing consultants, filling in forms and writing endless screeds of guess-at projections that you will have grossly neglected your farm; it will therefore have gone even deeper into debt than it was before, so he won't lend you the money anyway – that is, until you get things back to where they were before you started out on this paper chase.

If you do manage to get to the starting line, and don't by now feel you are on a hiding to nothing, now will be the time for your last long look, and to think very carefully, because from here on you will have probably committed yourself to debts, builders, planners and endless heartache, waiting for the day when whatever it is you have chosen to do will produce income, and start to reduce the borrowings. Most of us long enough in the tooth to have experience of this sort of carnage, remember that being at the mercy of these types can be pretty distressing, especially when things don't turn out quite right, or end up arriving a bit late – like, say 6 months. And the nice friendly business manager at the bank, who fifteen years ago replaced the nice friendly bank manger at the bank (who was at least allowed to think for himself, instead of having his strings pulled by head office, or computer programmes), turns into the nasty money lender from Victorian England, with his grubby fingers ready to pull the rug.

Don't go bleating on either, that no one told me, because I happen to farm in one of the most unattractive areas in the country, that holiday cottages wouldn't let here. Or – "we live down the end of a 2-mile narrow track, but the business consultant said it would be OK, because we could put up a board on the main road advertising our farm shop." In other words, if it scares you, don't do it; and don't rely on those smoothies, who are getting handouts to tell you what you should already know anyway, because if it goes belly up, and you are left holding the baby, they will have all cleared off with their fat fees, lining up ready to cash in on the next brilliant government brainwave to solve everyone else's problems.

Fortunately, as it happened, we didn't have to spend much money setting up our B&B. The local electrician was quite handy with a blow lamp and a copper pipe bender, so he soon had the wash basins in the bedrooms. The cost of extra linen, towels and other refinements were conjured up out of savings in the house-keeping budget; and it was too late in the season to advertise, so I just went round the other B&Bs in the district and asked them to pass onto us any extra guests they might have.

By the following year we were up and running, having paid back all our out of pocket expenses, and although we don't exactly live in the holiday heartland of the Cotswolds, it is pretty nice round here, and the Cotswold Way footpath passes right by us. – Bliss, ain't it? But you city slickers, who think you are going to make a killing by doing the same thing, and spending the rest of your lives in clover – don't bother, because shoe-string living is what you have to practise out here, and if you can't manage to get SINT MAXIMA EX MINIMIS (the maximum from the minimum) – (family motto) and are prepared to forgo endless holidays, or new cars, meals out, trips here, and theatres there, or this for the kids, and that for the wife, and heating turned up to the picture rails, or "shut that door" and "put that light out" sort of life, which if you were brought up as a kid on a shoe-string, is not that difficult anyway, and is, in the end, quite an acceptable way of life. Well, we're happy with it anyway. Some of our friends say I am tight – "Needs must," I tell them, but they still don't believe me. – Oh, well, I can't help that," and I quietly think to myself: "Like to see you trying it."

Having B&B people about can have its advantages, because after all, they are your eyes and ears if there is trouble and you're not there.

Charlie's head appeared over the garden wall. He had just come back from the local pub where he always went for his evening meal, and which he had been doing for a fortnight every summer on his annual visit to us. He came alone, and

spent every day, 6 1/2 days a week helping in a nearby archae-
ological dig on a Roman villa.

"There are a couple of kids firing air rifles at the cattle from
behind their garden wall, in the house down the lane," he
called. If anything makes me wild, it is people interfering or
endangering my stock. No sooner had I put my hoe down,
than I was in their garden, creeping up behind the two young
marksmen; and even as I quietly approached them – crack,
crack – two more shots were let off at poor old unsuspecting
Awel .

Grabbing both guns as simultaneously as I could, I wres-
tled them away from the kids, but of course, as one of them
struggled, he was struck in the face with his rifle butt.

By the time I was half way back up to the house again, carrying the confiscated guns, a burly Irish parent appeared in the
lane, bellowing after me, that he would be phoning the police.
Which meant I needed to get to the phone first to put my side
of the story. As he had a head start on me, because all he
needed to do was walk into his house and pick up the phone.
By the time I got to ours, we learnt later that he had succeeded, after which, the police had gone out, and I had got landed with their right hand man – the answering machine.

Of course we heard nothing until 11pm that night, when
we were in the kitchen, sorting things out before going to bed.
Suddenly there was an almighty banging on the kitchen window, looking up, we saw the angry face of a policeman staring
at us.

Some people have a nasty knack of putting themselves into
a confrontational position. This bloke had already walked past
two doors, both with bells and knockers on them; and had,
even so, managed to get himself round the back of the house
and then nearly frightened the living daylights out of us by his
sudden attack on our window. Having raised Pat's, the dog's
and my hackles, I fiercely gestured him back in the direction
from which he had just come. By the time he and I reached
the door he should have arrived at in the first place, the

description of me, which the Irish parent from down the lane probably gave him over the phone, must have fitted exactly: and we met head on in the doorway, like a couple of angry bulls.

Demanding entry, he marched in, quickly followed by a WPC and a Special, who had, unbeknown to us, been lurking about all the time, somewhere in the darkness behind him.

On several occasions now, I have noticed that some male officers of Her Majesty's Constabulary appear to have received their training at the hands of the SS, and being innocent until proved guilty is not a consideration for them. After the initial shouting and gesturing by the three of us (including Pat, although the other two officers kept well out of it) to establish the peck order. This young, flat eared twit (he had big ears flattened so hard against his head, I doubt he was ever able to wash behind them; and his mum, when he was young would never be able either to peel them from his head to establish if he had or he hadn't). This young man, who also had the appearance of having a constant smell under his nose, although that could have been me or the dog causing this disfigurement; eventually settled down.

Having heard the other side of the story, he thankfully went on his way, leaving the WPC and Special to take my statement. When both sides were satisfied, they, like everything in life, realised that coins have two sides, and that our first impressions of the departed officer had been correct; the WPC describing him as "always a bit like that", to our question concerning his manner. – They buzzed off, and we went to bed.

Just the same, I often wondered since, how big a part this chap's unusual ears played in his behaviour.

The WPCs we have ever had anything to do with during our life have been first class. Attentive, polite, considerate, and always kept us up to speed concerning the progress of the case. Of course the Irish parent down the lane was accusing me of assault on his son, and had the evidence of the bruised face, caused by the butt of the gun, if you remember – to prove it. Even so, after a couple of weeks had elapsed, the WPC was back telling us that no charges were to be brought either way; which to us was a bit of disappointment, because we don't feel kids should be allowed to go about taking pot-shots at livestock. Also, the bruised face was my word against the kid's, so as far as the law was concerned, that would be anyone's guess.

At the same time as giving us news of the decision, the WPC would no doubt have given it to the thuggish Irishman also, because within half an hour of her departure from us, the doorbell rang as if it was being torn from its seatings. We were expecting a B&B guest, and the three of us, (a friend was stay-ing for lunch), remarked on his seemingly desperate attempts to get into the place. By the time Pat had answered the door, I was immediately alerted to the situation by an Irish accent, (which had just spent the morning in the pub) asking for Mr. Forster. This visitor was not our B&B guest after all, but none other than the angry drunken Irish brute from down the road, obviously incensed that the police were to take no action against me, so he would square it for himself.

Quickly I got into the hall, and as I approached the open front door, I glanced past Pat, to see our man had come pre-pared, holding a thumb-stick in his right hand.
Slipping into the cloakroom as I went, I grabbed a walking stick. – No sooner had I re-emerged, than he pushed past Pat in a flash, and before I could raise my stick in defence, he landed a well-aimed, and I suspect, well exercised left hander to my eye, throwing me to the ground. And with that – made off.

This time it was my turn to be aggrieved, because once again, after a few weeks, there was a phone call from the local police sergeant, telling me that the C.P.S., in their wisdom, of which, of course, they haven't any, just simply a cash balance sheet – "wasn't taking any action, but I could take a private case against the perpetrator if I wished." "Thanks, that's good of them," I thought. – "What, in my state of wealth?"

If I hadn't known at the time that, within the next couple of weeks, the troublesome family from down the lane would be moving off to Bath, and we would be hopefully free of them forever, then I probably would have tried for a bit of justice in all this. After all, this lout had entered my house by force, and assaulted me. But I took solace in the fact, the less we had to do with them, the better, and they would soon be gone from us. At the same time, he had himself suffered at the hands of some pretty rough justice because upon learning where he had just been, on his return home from giving me a bashing, their next door neighbour told us later, that she heard over the hedge, his wife laying into him like nobody's business.

The B&B veggie guests are the ones I like best. You can't generally recognise them because they probably haven't been practising the art for that long, so it doesn't show too much. Pat, who is as honest as the day is long, has to tell me the truth, when I ask what everyone has ordered for tomorrow's breakfast.

Having got myself clued up; I always make sure I am looking round the stock in the field near the house as they set off on the next stage of their walk.

They have been our guests, and have paid us money after all, so you can't be too rough on them. There is also the danger that they may have some good medical reason for not eating meat. Anyway, we all have to live in this world together, and need to respect each other, and their different views. So my interest is, what might be described as purely educational.

Having established, by innocent conversation, which one it is, and then proceeded to answer all the questions about the cattle which inevitably follow. It is quite a simple matter to lead the conversation onto the type of farming which is practised all down the escarpment, which stretches the 100 mile length of the Cotswold Way; right from Chipping Campden, in the north, to Bath in the south; the path they have in fact been walking for the last 4 or 5 days, and will continue to walk for the next 3 or 4. The path which spends most of its time meandering across open grassland, with magnificent distant views over the Severn Vale and into Wales.

Here comes the punch line – because it is then, when they are telling me how they have enjoyed those beautiful views, and all about the wonderful scenery, that I ask the question. How do you think you would be able to see all this if cattle and sheep didn't graze these wild steep slopes along the scarp? For the only cattle who can cope with this poor grass are the beef cattle; and sheep were not kept for their near worthless fleeces, but to produce lamb; and the only alternative to that, if everyone were vegetarian, would be to grow trees, endless plantations of conifers and how would you see anything through them?

I never pretend to have ever converted anyone from vegetarianism, but I do enjoy the moment when they pause, obviously groping for the answer to my question, and then, as if in defeat, have to finally admit that they had never thought of that before.

If I was a youngster, a bit wild perhaps, I would probably go on my way leaping about and punching the air, but I'm not so inclined. I just content myself with having done something to try to redress the balance, and put a bit of sanity into the argument.

I'm afraid there was one occasion when I wasn't quite so gentle. It was at the time of the BSE crisis, when politicians all over the EU were really putting the boot into livestock farming in this country. The pathetic saga was practically at an end. We had got our act together, which was more than the other EU countries had done, but Germany was behaving in the usual protectionist way of that lot over the Channel, and refusing to take our beef. Our government, true to form was talking with wishy washy platitudes, (and I speak of all colours here); and there was no sense of urgency in dealing with the problem.

147

Because of the sleepy inertia of our lot, and the pig-headed attitude of the other lot, the British livestock farmers were beginning to lose patience, me amongst them. It was all I needed, when one afternoon, a couple stepped out of a car with foreign number plates, just as I arrived back at the house. They asked if we had any vacancies, which we had, and when I confirmed where they were from, you can imagine the way my mind began working, trying to sort out the next move.

Some of our self-righteous friends (a couple of females actually), when they learned about my response to this situation, told me I should have been more gracious, and were very surprised at my behaviour.

Even so, it wasn't as if we were the only B&B in the district. After all, there would be plenty of others who wouldn't have an axe to grind, and would take them, the sort who probably bought foreign meat anyway, if it meant saving a few bob.

Having said that, before I sent them on their way, I did make absolutely certain they knew I wasn't getting at them personally, but I wanted them to go back home and complain to their government about the way they were straining Anglo German relationships (I don't suppose for a minute they did, but it was worth a try). But like so many stories, there was one small crumb of comfort. Credit due, they did try to pour oil on troubled waters, even if it was somewhat misguided, by saying that I shouldn't worry, because they were vegetarians anyway!

It's not the people of the other EU countries I have disagreement with, but their governments, because it seems in practically every country the ordinary people don't want all this close integration. In fact, I am convinced there is a growing number who are now saying, we must come out of Europe completely. They have had enough of this all-powerful merry band of unelected bureaucratic thugs, stifling and strangling the lifeblood from us, by their extravagancies and evermore-burdensome regulations. For no other reason than to give them – them the perpetrators, an even greater feeling of power. Although, one day, during the German beef blockade, I did happen to meet an apparently ordinary person who appeared not to share that anti feeling.

"No we're not Dutch, we're German," I heard a woman's voice saying to the man behind the counter of an upmarket mobile fish & chip bar, parked a few yards behind me, as I sat gazing out to sea while I waited for Pat who had gone shopping. We were on holiday in Hugh Town on the Isles of Scilly.

Discreetly I turned my head towards the sound and watched as the voice and, (I suppose, although you never know these days), her husband approached the seat next to mine. Soon they had settled themselves down, and were tucking into the contents of their paper bags like true Englishmen.

"So you like our fish & chips better than our beef then, do you?"

The reaction to my question was quite startling really, the scrabbling around in the paper bags stopped immediately; and before long we were engaging in battle. Thank goodness he didn't say much, because she was obviously fighting for a cause in which she had great conviction.

I shan't bore you with the detail partly because I can't remember it all. But the thing which really convinced me that she had been thoroughly brainwashed by the system, was when she told me. "You need us" – I couldn't believe that anyone could possibly have been so persuaded of the benefits of this unscrupulous gluttonous EU monster as to utter those words, to an Englishman, especially.

Needless to say, I told them we needed them like a hole in the head, and suggested, that when they got back to Penzance, where they had left their motor-caravan, they took the trouble to stand on the side of the road for a few minutes, and see how many BMW, Mercedes, Volkswagen and Audi motor cars passed them; and then she could ask herself the question. Who really needs whom? Despite the fracas the three of us parted on good terms. They having enough trust in me to ask where the cliff path led if they took it,

I can only assume she must have been on the Brussels' pay-roll though.

As well as educational conversations – that is – them learn-ing about us, and what goes on out here, we do get educated about them too. So here are a few tips from our experiences for the uninitiated who might be thinking of doing B&B.

If you get Americans visiting always go out and buy a pig first; otherwise you will soon have difficulty in coping with all the waste from their plates. And giving them less each day won't help either, because however little you give them, they will always manage to leave some.

I believe it's a digestive disease known as affluence.

Don't let anyone go off for the day leaving the kids behind, no matter how nice and well behaved they seem; because soon they will do daft things like sitting on the wash basins. And if there aren't two of them, there won't be anyone to come and tell you what has happened, if one has to stay there holding up the offending basin in her arms, to stop all the plumbing being torn off the wall, and flooding the place.

If the phone rings waking you up in the early hours, don't answer it, because it is likely to be a relative of one of your guests phoning to let them know that their old aunt has just died, something they had been expecting to happen for weeks, so it wasn't that much of a surprise. Then, when you are left hovering about on the landing in your dressing gown, waiting for an explanation, don't be surprised if, when they return to their room after taking the phone call, they walk straight past you as if you weren't there. This will probably make you think that, just because you have been woken out of your sleep; why should you then think that it is any of your business anyway? Don't expect either, an explanation at breakfast, because they will soon tell you that instead of staying for a week, which they had booked, they will be leaving straightaway, even though they have only been here for two days.

Having by now realised you have here a couple of incon-siderate morons, you can't wait to get them out through the door soon enough, even though they haven't paid for the remaining five days of their booking.

You need to trust people, because it can be to your advantage.

If guests are breaking their journey with you, they sometimes leave very early the next morning. We never saw a father and a son who stayed with us for one night. They came when we happened to be out, having received their entry instructions over the phone, and left before we were up – not stopping for breakfast either, but obligingly leaving their money on the hall table.

If old ladies complain incessantly, ignore them. Two of our regular visitors, who came year after year were a Mr and Mrs White. He was small and never said much; she was large with a loud voice, wore a straw hat, and was eccentrically charming; but always managed to throw in a complaint amongst the conversation. On one occasion he did succeed in grabbing everyone's attention when we happened to hear splashing water coming from the other side of our front door as he frantically fumbled with his key, trying to get in. Our worst fears were founded when he eventually appeared in the doorway with wet trousers. Although these fears were soon turned to relief, after we noticed he was carrying a lidless Thermos flask upside-down.

Make sure your guests know thoroughly the workings of your door locks, and that they fully understand what you are saying about them. Otherwise they might have to spend the evening, well into the night with your neighbours because you happen to have gone visiting friends.

Don't be alarmed by guests who come down to breakfast flustered, with stories of enormous creatures in their bedroom, which due to their fortitude, they had managed to capture under the upturned waste paper basket. The chances are, it will be a largish spider, and don't let your amusement show when they excuse themselves by saying they are unused to that sort of thing, because they come from the city.

Watch out for the nervous driver. They are the ones who won't be staying the course round the country lanes; and will have to return home sooner than expected, because they feel a nervous breakdown coming on.

Don't show your concern too much, it might disillusion the wife of the guest who has just dropped, clutching his chest, and writhing in agony, to the floor. When at your suggestion, that you should call a doctor; she replies that "Oh no, he'll be alright, our doctor said he's better now."

Watch out for the wedding guests; they'll take you over, especially if there are more than two; and sometimes they get back late the worse for wear. Although we have, thank goodness, never had that experience.

They also arrive early in the morning before you have even had chance to do their rooms, expecting to kick around the place, getting in everyone's way, wanting to change their clothes, and then go about parading like cock pheasants, as if no one ever got married anymore (which most don't, I suppose).

We had four who turned up one day with a misbehaving car. They spent the morning on our phone between ringing the AA, all their parents, and I think, just about everyone in their address books. I spent the morning hunting for a pair of my long forgotten cuff links, because one of the blokes had come away without his. Then most of the afternoon assisting the AA chap with their misbehaving car.

Boy - were we glad to see the back of them. That was when we decided. "No more wedding guests."

Make sure you get a worthwhile deposit; and even that won't cover you if they don't turn up at all; especially if you have just turned someone else away.

One considerate soul did have the courtesy to phone us from Bristol on the night they were supposed to be arriving with us, to say they had met some friends and would be staying with them instead. When Pat told him she thought that was not good enough, he retorted. That he could change his mind if he wanted to. "And how would you feel," she barked, "if you had arrived at our door after booking a room, and I told you, we had let it to someone else, because I could change my mind if I wanted to?"

If you only let a couple of rooms, you really do need to have a strict timetable, such as breakfast at 8.30am – no messing, otherwise, you could end up by doing breakfasts all the morning.

Four French had booked in – they would be visiting friends in the next village, and would be along at about midnight, so we arranged for them to have a key. At about 10pm they phoned to say. Would we mind if they came at 2 am? How do you say: "Yes, we do mind." Instead you remind them that breakfast is at 8.30am, and hope they get the message.

8.30am comes and goes. 9am comes and so does one of the guests. "Where are the rest?" the landlady inquires, beginning to bristle a bit, like all good landladies should if they intend keeping an orderly house. "Oh, they will be down in about one hour," comes the reply. From then on he said he had difficulty in understanding Pat's English. Things soon changed when she suddenly snapped. "No, Vite" (quick)

He turned and fled upstairs, returning with the other three in a flash.

Make sure all your electrical appliances are in good working order.

We returned one evening after being out for a couple of hours to discover the burnt-out wreck of our TV in the garden.

Be careful of workman guests, they get bored in the evenings, and could drink too much.

A friend of ours who also did B&B had a couple – nice chaps – after they had gone; she noticed a puddle under one of the beds.

It wasn't because he'd missed the guzzunder. – It was more that he hadn't bothered to get out of the bed.

Shortly after replacing the bed and mattress with new ones,

she had a phone call from them to book another couple of nights!

None of these stories are too horrific (except the last one, which didn't happen to us – although the wash-basin could have been tricky) and that is in about thirty years of doing B&B. So don't be put off, because, compared with all the good stories I could tell, and which you wouldn't want to hear anyway, because good stories are boring. I think on balance the good times outweigh the bad ones.

It's something like that lot over the Channel I suppose – if they want to sell all those motor cars every year. – "they need us."

Or, unless you're going to spend the night under canvas; without soaking in a lovely hot bath, and lying in a comfortable warm bed after a long day tramping the Cotswold Way; then you are going "To Need Us" – And of course. – We need your money.

CHAPTER 13

Why Are They With Us For Such a Short Time?

Sian.

"Blue merle? What's blue merle?" I asked, as the breeder told me, in answer to my telephone call that he had only Welsh Border Collies left with those markings.

When we got to his kennels and peered into the pen we were convinced that blue merle would be just fine: and have been convinced ever since – Three dogs and twenty-nine years later.

"Have a bitch, they don't go off like dogs," some bright spark once told us. So we did, despite always having unneutured dogs without too much of a problem when I was young and still at home.

"Which should we have?" I asked our two boys, as the mass of black, white and grey (merle, white and blue) romped about the pen with each other. "They all look the same, don't they? Except that one – she's got a fat tummy, let's have that one – she's different", one of the boys retorted.

I never could remember which of them it was who said that! Of course, we should have known better than to use that as a reason for choosing a dog.

"We've got your dog here." It was years later, and simply an extension in the endless saga of the wanderings of that blooming dog who could smell food a mile away. Chocolate food at newsagents. School dinner, food at the local comprehensive. Bread rolls food at the bakery. Breakfast food at the hotel. The voice on the phone was the chef at the breakfast food. "She's been here all night again, sleeping outside my bedroom door," he quipped, obviously amused at the devoted admiration of this female.

"Why don't you tie her up when you're working in the garden," Pat snapped at me, and by now, well and truly fed up with all the phone calls from long suffering people who had found Sian, either turning up in their kitchens, or following them back home because of the food in their shopping baskets. Of course, she was right; and perhaps I was being a bit stubborn, but I really was hoping to train her to stay with me when I was working. In the end the. "I want a dog to stay with me all the time without being forced to," wore a bit thin and I had to give up, and admit defeat.

Even so, there was one memorable occasion when she escaped, and I wasn't to blame.

"We've been burgled, could someone come round, please." – I was on the phone to the local police station. So they did – they sent three of them - one morning. The back door was unlocked, and we signalled through the kitchen window for them to come on in.

Now it would be the first constable who must have opened the door; and he would have been followed through it by the second, and then by the third: who I suppose, because he hadn't opened the door in the first place, didn't shut it either, and Sian who hadn't been out by that time of the morning, so she didn't have her collar and name tag on, - spotted, unbeknown to us – or them – an opportunity for extra food.

Being pre-occupied with the break-in, and the combined resourses of what must have been about half the Gloucestershire Constabulary, it was several hours before we were aware that she had slipped off, by which time, the culprits of the open door had gone on their way too. Pity really, because it would have been a great treat to watch someone else getting a wigging instead of me. Anyway, the bloke who got the wigging was the sergeant who answered the phone at the police station when Pat reported the escaped dog, and how it had happened.

"So if you get a collie bitch brought in without a collar it will be ours" she commanded.

"Yes" he understood, "and of course you won't be prosecuted under the circumstances for allowing a dog without any means of identification to wander off," he informed her.

I think he was rather glad to be able to give her some good news after this last remark; which was a bit like showing a lighted match to a barrel of gunpowder. For he quickly went on to say that someone had just brought in a collie bitch fitting her description, but who was also heavy in pup. "was yours heavy in pup?" he asked.

"No, that will be food which is having that effect,' Pat replied.

It wasn't until she arrived at the police station, and got the sergeant to feel the dog's stomach for himself and, by doing so, identified the contents as unmistakably that of bridge rolls, that he was convinced she wasn't pregnant after all! And, if he had been sitting in the car on the journey home, he would have been even more convinced: when suddenly she regurgitated the lot back onto the floor, absolutely complete in every way in both shape and size.

Having a bitch for the first time, in fact having a bitch at all has its down side.

Looking out through the landing window one morning as I came down the stairs; I was a bit surprised to see, gazing

157

intently at our yard door beneath, a couple of rows of dogs sitting in the copse opposite. Their concentration was such that they didn't even notice me watching them, and although they were a pretty motley bunch, they all seemed quite happy to sit amongst each other without so much as a quarrel between them.

Now, in all the years we had been living in the house, I had never before noticed all the strays and wanderers of the district gathered in one place; and especially outside our door, but what was even more striking was the sense of serenity hanging over that group of observers and the peaceful expressions on all the faces. What, I thought, could possibly be the cause of this unusual phenomenon? The answer wasn't far behind the question – Sex! – got it in one, I thought – Not only could I never remember which of our two boys had suggested we had "the one with the fat tummy." I never remembered either who the bright spark was who said that we should have a bitch.

So, here we are, landed with another problem, half the dogs in the neighbourhood hanging about the place; and when it gets dark tonight, I suppose they'll all be out there howling too: and that wasn't all. Pat generally liked to have a walk in the morning, with what had now become the centre of attraction for all the boys from everywhere. So it wasn't too difficult to imagine now, how the walk over the next few days would progress; or maybe process, and I couldn't resist a chuckle to myself, as this picture emerging in my mind of Pat walking nonchalantly along, pretending not to notice Sian, trotting behind, followed closely by a riotous mob of ruffian dogs, each jockeying for a better sniff at the scent.

As it happened, being a bit resourceful – Pat had a plan. When she was about to go out, she popped Sian on the lead, opened the yard door, waited a few moments for all the merry men to come rushing down from the copse, scrambling past her, and our bitch – straight into the yard – whereupon, she promptly shut the door with them on the inside, and her and our bitch on the outside: and set off for her walk unmolested.

"As we're putting up with all this trouble, we might as well make it worth our while and try and get her in pup." I suggested. "but not with any old dog. Can't we find a nice collie about somewhere?" I added – and, as luck would have it, who should turn up in the woods one day whilst the mob were impounded in our yard and Pat was having a nice peaceful walk, but the dog from the neighbouring farm. A smart young collie chap - and with very little encouragement from Pat, it wasn't too long before he obliged! . But the problem then was, unlike the bull - as quick as a flash and it's all over - dogs are different , which was something I had observed from an early age, with great interest and surprise. Although apparently, Pat had not, being of sheltered upbringing and shyness of character, (she probably must have looked the other way, I suppose).

So there she was, stuck up in the woods, hanging about, hiding away her embarrassment behind a tree in case anyone should come along. Waiting there, while these two tried to sort themselves out again.

As it was, it didn't work, which we were rather glad about because we decided there were too many dogs around anyway. After that experience Sian had obviously been put off too, because whenever a dog approached her with seemingly sinister intentions, she would bare her teeth and chase him off. Even that didn't need to last for much longer either, because about the time we thought it might be prudent to have her spayed in case she attacked and killed one of her besotted admirers. (Something like a female spider does to the bloke who's just served her) – she stopped causing any more of the problems, and completely switched off – so to speak.

Of course that meant I had then to turn round and drastically reduce the size of the rather handsome wooden bed I had just completed for her and her once expected litter.

"Well, the trouble is, sometimes, if a bitch has never had pups, the chances are she could develop cancer of the mammary glands," said the vet, looking up from his examination of Sian. "we could operate if it's non-malignant, even though she's 13 years old – she's a fit animal, and could go on for quite a while yet" he added.

By the time we had accepted that we should never take our eyes off this dog, in case she wandered away with a bunch of people she had befriended, and we had also got past the problem of her fatal attraction for the men folk of the district; our bond with her had become immensely strong. Like so many collies she was affectionate and adoring: as we were towards her. So the news from the vet was rather a bombshell, but we clung to the bright bit – "If it's non-malignant" – Which cheered us up.

According to the autopsy it was non-malignant, so we went ahead with the operation, and for a bit all was well.

Unfortunately this turned out to be a false dawn, because not many months had passed before it was back somewhere else, with secondaries in her brain. This time there was nothing more we could do, only make sure she didn't suffer, but as time went on, periods between her petit mals grew shorter, until Pat began to say that I should take her to the vet's and have her put to sleep. Of course, as usual she was right. – But how was I going to bring myself to do this? Then, one day, after another attack, followed by Pat's usual response, I retorted in desperation: "Well, why don't you take her!" But, thank goodness, as it happened, it didn't befall either of us. Because, before the end of that day poor old Sianie passed quietly away.

Gosh – How I missed that dog.

Jack

People always say, after you have lost one of these great friends. "You must get another straight away, and then the loss won't seem so bad." Well, they're probably right I suppose, but to me it seems rather disrespectful to the one who has just gone, and even if it was "only a dog", as some might say, they are often amongst those closest to you, and your grief is very real. I think it would be something like trying to rush their memory and your sadness out of your life, so that you can forget them, and be preoccupied with other things, as if they never happened, but they did happen, every day they happened – they were always there, waiting for you – being with you – part of you. How can part of you be taken away just like that, and you be expected to get straight on with your life again?

So we waited. I don't remember for how long we waited, but it must have been long enough to get over the loss, but of course, not the memory.

"Do you know – I don't reckon we're going to be able to get another blue merle." I said to Pat and the boys. (Boys? Chaps by now I suppose at 20 and 17 years old.) , as we returned from a wild goose chase round the farms on north Somerset, where someone had told Peter, our eldest that she had heard of a litter of blue merle pups, but couldn't quite remember the name of the farm.

Becoming resigned, I said to everyone's great disappointment. "perhaps we should settle for a black and white; there's a litter on a farm near Dursley." Then having a rush of inspiration, I added. "Let me just pop next door, Len and June will have an Evening Post, you never know what might be advertised in there." So I did – and there was. – "Black and white collies, some blue merles." On a farm about 15 miles away, towards Bristol.

"Can we come over straightaway?" I asked the wife at the other end of the phone. Within the hour she was busy bringing the pups into her kitchen for us to inspect.

"There are just the two blue merle dogs" she proudly announced and proud she should be too: both beautifully marked, although neither with wall eyes as Sian had. (A walleye is pale blue with a large amount of white showing, some people mistake it for blindness. It can be safely said though that the condition is far from that), but walleyes are quite common in blue merles.

Both these dogs had deep brown eyes, and looked as if they were going to have shorter coats that Sian.

"Which one is it going to be then?" I asked, hoping not to have an answer from the other three, and I didn't; they couldn't decide, but I had, in my mind already. "Let's have the one with the black patch on his back," I suggested – they all agreed – Done!

"I don't think we should have that one after all Dad", whispered Peter, as the wife disappeared from the room to take the other pups back – "His breath smells" – bit late now I thought. We all leaned forward to test his observations – and withdrew pretty smartish – "Crumbs, he's right" I said. "Never mind, it'll be worms."

Just as soon as we could get the tablets into him Jack was thoroughly wormed; and within a few days they started to come away – masses and masses of little white roundworms, wrapped around each other like tangled balls of wool. How any food was left for the poor little chap after that lot had finished with it, was a miracle: or how much longer, he himself could have survived that sort of infestation was an even bigger question? After a short while of treating and watching, the all clear came; and as the worms vanished, so did the nasty breath.

Poor Jack was born with only one parent; not that he would notice I suppose. It must happen in lots of cases. A wayward bitch and an opportunist dog, who then promptly disappears into the distance, never to be seen again. Although the suspicions would always be there, depending on how the pups looked when they came out or even more: as they grew up. You can imagine it, can't you? – "That's that blasted greyhound from over the Wilson's I bet", someone, one day would say as it suddenly struck them when the greyish, brownish, blackish assorted pups out of the black labrador bitch grew ever more leggy and skinny, but with Jack it was different, and, of course, proper. His mum was the blue merle, and his dad, the black and white, both collies, and both living at home in respectable circumstances. Then one day, during his mother's confinement, Jack, his dad, was run over and killed.

We always wondered about this, whether it could have had any bearing on young Jack's great fear of motor vehicles. As soon as he heard one approaching, he would make an immediate dive for the hedge, or scramble high onto the roadside bank, well clear of them as they passed by, and he never really did enjoy a trip out in the car, even after he had got over his early bout of car sickness. It was always under great sufferance that he would persuade himself to jump into the car, realising that he would have to endure this time of persecution to have the reward of the walk at the other end of the journey. But then, that sounds like superstition. How could the circumstances of the death of an unborn dog's father possibly have any influence on that dog? – Funny though wasn't it?

Some dogs never seem to manage to get trained. - Some dogs seem to get half trained. – Some could get trained if their owners had got trained first. Then there are the other dogs; the dogs that got trained in their mother's womb. Jack was one of these. After being with us for a couple of days, after his – so far – long 8 weeks life, he was standing in the kitchen next to Pat as she prepared our food. Just to see what would happen, I told him to sit, without so much as a glance towards me, without a glimmer of hesitation whatsoever. – He did – immediately. "Fluke!" I hear you saying; but it wasn't, because he always did it, every time – from then on.

"Instinct – it's born in them" – How often do we hear that explanation for the way a dog is; and yet no one can quite explain it. Collies I think are the best example of this. Is it hundreds of years herding stock, that the habit becomes instilled in the blood, and which we call instinct? It's something generations of shepherds must have puzzled about, but there are still no answers, and I hope there never will be; at least, not in my lifetime anyway. Mystery is a wonderful thing: knowledge and calculated explanation can be so boring.

"These wretched cows, how am I ever going to get them on the hill?" I shouted to myself, or to them, who were being so unco-operative. It was a shout of sheer desperation.

We calve down near the house on the good pasture in May and June, and then move all the cows with their newborn calves onto the hill after they have calved, and where the grass is the much poorer tor grass, but they don't like it, and will do all they can to stop me getting them up there. That was before we decided to keep the black cattle from Wales, who don't care too much what they eat, as long it can be digested. Before that change, we were running Hereford cross Friesian cows, who most certainly did care about what we tried to get them to stuff into their bellies.

The trick on these occasions with getting the HxF onto the hill was to run an electric fence right up from the bottom of the field to the gate at the top of that field, which then led out onto the hill. Hopefully, if everything went to plan the cows would keep going, being driven by me from the rear, and kept in place to the one side by the electric fence. When you got them to the gate, it was a simple matter then to just guide them through.

The problem we were having now was that after a few years of these tactics every summer, the cows had grown wary of where it was all leading them. They found if they were quick enough, they could double back past me. This then was the stage I was at today, with cows getting one over on me.

Convinced I had lost the battle, I was on the verge of going back down to fetch Pat to give me a hand, but what I hadn't noticed was a little 12-week-old observer, who had been brought out on his first adventure, as a special treat. Just as I was about to turn round and go back down for help, I was suddenly aware that the cows were no longer attempting to double back; but that they were walking on in an orderly fashion; and here on my right was the explanation. Every time one of these half-ton beasts attempted to make a run for it, this little presence was there, chasing them back in line again.

Instilled with renewed confidence by my young helper, the two of us bashed on together, and in next to no time the whole bunch of stroppy power crazed creatures had been disciplined into co-operating with us, and were off through the gate and safely onto the hill.

Well then, if that wasn't instinct and basic common sense wrapped up in enduring mystery, what else will you be calling it?

Although the basic skills and in-born ways are there in a good collie dog, they are in a relatively rough – hewn form, left by God; maybe for man to be allowed to add his touch, with a final polish; so that he can feel he has, in some small but painstaking way, contributed to the delightful creature who emerges from a partnership between the divine and the earthly. Something in the way of a diamond I suppose. Even so, it is not everyone who is able to share in such a partnership, for they too will need the skills to expose and develop what has been placed in the animal before him; and to draw out the best that lies buried there.

I am afraid that this is where most of us who attempt to create a man and dog working relationship are left. Not being able to polish the stone to its full brilliance, but having to be content with a slight smoothing of its rough edges, and just hoping to get by. So it was quite sad for me, because of my shortcomings, to recognise a good dog, whose full potential still lay untapped within him, and, because of my inadequacies, I would never be able to release. – That dog was Jack.

Having a dog, despite being unpolished, did, even so make life a lot easier. A dog working with cattle needs to be just that little bit bolder than one working with sheep. He needs to be able to stand and "eye" his quarry; and it is often a battle of nerves between a stubborn cow and a determined dog. But whatever happens, the dog must not give in; he must somehow or other move that giant on to wherever it is she or he (if a bull) or it (if a steer) is meant to be. This "eyeing" process can take several minutes sometimes; with the dog-stalking round the cow hoping to unnerve her; and the cow following the intense stare of the eye of the dog, with her own.

At times, the cow will attempt to charge the dog, and the dog, if he is good, will have none of it, and will seize the opportunity to turn the tables, and get his way, or the dog may just get fed up with stalking round the cow, and then suddenly make a dive for her back feet, taking her unawares. Whereupon the dog has won the battle again; as the cow, having started to move, will then go chasing off to join the rest. The most peaceful way though, is for the cow to realise that she has met her match in seeing the dog's determination, and just quietly walk off to where she should be.

Jack was good at these tactics – determined, and completely unafraid of cattle; he would take on all comers – but what he couldn't cope with was me getting cross, and shouting at him if he didn't get things right. Should this happen, and I had to learn very quickly not to let it, because immediately it did, he would stop what he was doing, and skulk off home, and no amount of gentle talk and persuasion could get him back again. – I had lost, and had to finish the job by myself.

Naturally, all collies like a good chase, no matter what it is, just as long as it moves. Jack's spare time hobbies were chasing hot-air balloons, lights and shadows. Hot-air balloons he obviously reckoned he was pretty good at, because, being hilly round here, he generally managed to chase them off, what he must have thought was the end of the world, because, after about 5 minutes and 1/2 mile the thing would disappear away over the hill, out of sight, and he would return elated, and wearing his wide grin, which he saved for all his great achievements.

Lights were produced by a torch sending a beam, whether in the house or outside. Outside was the best because with a powerful beam he would run all over the hillside, and come back completely exhausted. Inside, torches produced skating mats, along with anything else which was movable, and which stood in the way of the performing light, and the flying dog.

Shadows: any shadow, provided it moved would give him endless entertainment with his leaping and pouncing, in trying to secure the thing to the ground; only to find it had moved on somewhere else.

I suppose he must have realised sooner or later, that what he spent so much of his spare time doing could never achieve anything worthwhile, like getting a bunch of cattle where you wanted them; so it was simply just a game, and he must have been content with that. – No different from twenty two blokes wasting their time bashing a ball about, and another few thousand, slating or encouraging them for doing it.

This dog was a strange mixture; on the one hand he was remarkably fearless with the stock, and yet quite sensitively nervous, and easily upset on the other. But a better companion and chum a chap could never wish to have. The sort of fella you could have endless conversations with, just you and him, out there away from it all, and although he was never able to reply to what you were saying to him; he conveyed a great sense of understanding through his expressions, which were always so very readable.

It was because of this enormously strong bond between us, that the first realisation that something was very wrong with him had a profound affect on me.

Barely ten years old, the first indication of this, was one day as we were returning with some friends from a walk; suddenly we were aware that he was no longer with us. I went back to look for him, and found him round a bend in the lane, wandering about in a daze, going round in circles, and with a glazed look in his eyes. He eventually came to, and although not his usual self, walked back with me to the house.

Clutching at straws, as we all do when trying to dismiss unpleasant things, we assumed he had picked up something, and was suffering from a mild attack of poisoning, and decided, if he was back to his old self the next day, that that would be what it was, and there would be no need to do anything further. As it happened, the next day he was back to normal

167

again, and with great relief, life continued as before. Until a week or two later – another attack. So it wasn't poison after all.

"I'm afraid he has a lump here," said the vet; and sure enough, when I felt Jack's stomach, there was something pretty substantial growing there.

After the operation, which a good friend of ours insisted on paying for: a friend, who very sadly, even as I write, died only the other day from cancer. Jack returned home, having had the lump, and part of his bowel removed, and with the good news that the thing was non-malignant. With the heavy lump gone from his side, he now had a tendency to walk a little off balance for a while, until he was able to compensate for its absence again.

Even so, it seemed no time at all before we were going over that old familiar ground again. The strange wandering about, the vacant expression: the abnormal behaviour; and the little turns all growing in their frequency.

"Unfortunately, this time I'm afraid there is nothing more we can do, only to make sure he doesn't suffer," was as we expected, the vet's verdict. Then one day, Jack didn't want to come out with me to see the cattle; and I knew the time had arrived. The end of the road had been reached.

The vet, that day was on a routine visit to see some of the stock, but before he did, he came to the house. As I held Jack close to me where he lay peacefully under the kitchen table, the tiny needle was gently pressed into his foreleg; the syringe softly pushed the half-inch of its length; and Jack's eyes quietly closed.

He had gone – No longer would we be together over the hill. No longer would I see his happy smiling face; his welcome every morning; our long conversations – The shadow, even on a sunless day. – He had gone. – How was it, in just half an inch of a syringe, could there have been such a final and devastating effect? The vast gulf between life and death had been spanned in a second there, under our kitchen table.

That gulf, from which there could never be any return, had left me on my own, and he had gone from me forever.

I buried him under a holly tree in a quiet corner of the garden, and it was so hard digging that grave; but no dog of mine had ever been buried by anyone else; and dear Jack would definitely not be.

As we laid him in the bottom of that quiet spot, wrapped safely in his blanket, these words kept returning to me, the words that I had so often spoken to him throughout his short life. Words, which had always been so true, right back as far as I could remember: but were even more so now that he was no longer here. These words, thought through my tears – "the best little fella a fella could want."

Even now, in my quiet times, I still have difficulty coping with those last memories of him.

He would be only sixteen now, if he had lived – but then I would have had him with me longer, and that, I suppose would have made those last moments even harder.

Bryn

"What do you do now?" I used to think to myself – no dog, surely is going to measure up to that one. So it wouldn't be fair on the new one to be constantly compared with the other. It was therefore a long, long time before we were convinced that each dog, like each person, will be different from the next, and each must be looked upon and treated as an individual but, even so, nothing quite prepared us for what was to come.

"Don't talk to me about that litter," said a desperate sounding shepherd, who had just been reminded of a very unpleasant experience, which he would have preferred to have forgotten: and he wasn't the only desperate one either, because one year earlier we had bought a pup out of that litter, and I was on the phone to him hoping for words of comfort, and helpful advice.

"I kept one of the bitches out of that litter, to run with my other dogs," he went on. Now, if a chap knew his sheep dogs, he did, and if a chap knew how to train sheep dogs, he did, because he had been doing it for a very long time, and was responsible, with his six dogs for a large flock of sheep on the Ragley Hall Estate near Evesham.

"It got so bad with this bitch," he added, "that I was seriously thinking of shooting her – I have never had such a difficult dog. She did just as she wanted to, scattering the sheep, ignoring me, ignoring the other dogs. There was nothing I could do to control her – she was absolutely wild. I was upsetting the other dogs with all my shouting; and then, in a last desperate attempt I decided to pen her up every day. So that when the others went off to work with me in the truck, she was left behind, and only let out again in the evenings, to join the rest in their game of football."

He continued – "after six weeks I thought I would try her; and she was a changed dog. Now I wouldn't part with her for £2000."

"Well," I thought to myself. Do I take this as reassurance or hopelessness? After all, I couldn't measure up to his abilities as a trainer of collies: and if he had trouble coping, what chance do we have? As it happened, I looked on this tale of woe with the happy ending, and remembered just the happy ending bit, and decided to persevere, and five years later we're still persevering, and getting there. But perhaps that is probably a little unfair towards Bryn, because although it took us four years to teach him to be a proper dog, and not a rebel, the cattle dog bit came soon afterwards.

I suppose though, if you have only just two blue merle dog pups to choose from, which we did when we visited the shepherd and his new litter, then you have to hope you have decided for the right reasons, on the right dog.

"He's the bolder of the two," was the shepherd's reply to our, "What's the difference?" question.

"Well, I suppose Jack was bold with the cattle, but easily upset with so many other things, such as traffic; riding in the car, me shouting at him – or anything else; and airliners flying overhead at 20,000 ft which, I must confess, are beginning to get at me a bit these days too. Considering we have all this electronic gadgetry – what on earth are all these people doing jetting off across the Atlantic on expense accounts for? Can you believe, that in this country of ours, where we need heat to survive the winters, these idiot politicians have put a tax on heat and light, and yet at the same time have let the airlines, which are just involved mainly in the luxury trade, of taking people on holiday, and so-called company executives on firm jollies – off scot free of any tax?

"Tax the blighters out of the sky" I say. –

But then I digress – but you see my point!

So stupidly, we had the bolder of the two dogs, didn't we? And, although he was the perfect gentleman about the house, practically right from the start, except. – We always did, and still do, on occasions have this problem of him mucking up the floor in the boiler room. (Thank goodness it is concrete, and we can just give it a good sluice down), this happens whenever he decides to supplement his meals with a diet of rabbit droppings, dried cow pats; or his delicacy: baby calf-milky-whey-dung, and boy doesn't the last one produce some shockingly devastating effects. But outside he is horrific.

Bryn's first visit to the cattle was when he was 12 weeks old, (about the same age as Jack would have been when he helped me herd the cows onto the hill). We walked into the field to check them over. No sooner through the gate than he was gone; fortunately very few of the cows took any notice of this little freak scuttling about amongst them, and complete-ly out of control; but from then on, for what seemed an age, I always had to walk about the place with him on the end piece of a baler twine – it was the only way any of us got any peace.

This overwhelming power, as I have come to call it, mani-fests itself in open spaces, and the effects can be quite dra-matic; something like lifting the traps on a line of greyhounds when the hare is set off.

171

Take for example the evening we arrived home after a trip out in the car: he, I suppose would have been about twelve months old by then. As I lifted the tailgate to let him out, suddenly there was a flash which shot past me into the darkness of the night. Two hours later we had a phone call saying he was on the doorstep of a house where the occupants thought their bitch might possibly be coming on heat. We have never had need to get any of our dogs neutered before that.

By the time we had reached the end of the following day, so had Bryn's sex life. If the vet had said he wasn't able to fit him in before then, I think I would have resorted to the two bricks method, so desperate had we become in attempting to bring a vestige of control into this dog's life, that we felt we couldn't cope with these sorts of diversions as well.

I suppose the confirmation of this dog's wild nature was, as he grew older, one day I noticed that one of his ears, which until then had been resting peacefully flopped over this head, as most collies ears do; now and again began to lift itself into the upright position; or "pricked", as they are known. This was quickly followed within a week, by the other ear. As the force, whatever it was, developed strength in his ears, this force also appeared to develop strength within the dog. So that by the time the two ears were fully "pricked", giving the appearance of not just alertness, but more worryingly, absolute wilfulness, he grew correspondingly, even more wild!

Although surprisingly, whilst all the devastation was happening within and around him, his loving nature towards us and everyone else, was becoming even more acute than before. It was as if he were constantly seeking forgiveness from us for all his wicked ways.

No matter how I shouted and raved when we were outside together, he just continued to do exactly as the overwhelming power from within compelled him to. I was, and still am convinced that he had been completely taken over by this force. The same genes and hormones that were causing his ears to go pricked, I was sure, instilled in the rest of him, this uncontrollable state.

The question was How to deal with it? We hadn't got here the same means, which the shepherd from Ragley Hall had to affect a cure. Bryn wouldn't feel out of things when the other dogs went off for the day, because we hadn't got any other dogs. So all we were left with was perseverance: or getting rid of him, and we didn't want to inflict all this misery on anyone else. This meant, getting rid of him would have to simply mean, just that – off the face of the earth.

One day I made the fatal mistake of telling a neighbour, an old lady, that we were getting towards the end of the road with him; and that might have to be the result. – Crumbs, didn't she go for me? After that, I just kept quiet, except in the privacy of our own home, where I knew I could count on Pat's sympathy – although even she was becoming weary with my constant complaining every time I came in after being out with this pest for a few hours.

Anything, which moved, got chased. Birds, squirrels, foxes, rabbits, cats, people, our cattle. (we kept him right away from other people's: he would have got shot, and that was an option we were keeping up our sleeve) – horses and cars – the last one caused the greatest problems.

Cars were a speciality of his; and he didn't have to be anywhere near them to start the chase. The nearest I dared get to a road without the bailer twine round his neck was about 400 yards. Although, judging from the number of times he disappeared into thin air, and was next reported to be chasing about amongst the traffic, I think half a mile would have been a safer distance.

Looking back on all this never seems as bad, except when we see photographs of the two of us (Pat and me, that is), before he stormed into our lives. When we look at ourselves now, somehow or other there seems to have been a considerable ageing process, which has overtaken us during those few years.

How he is still alive six years later, I can't understand,

because if I hadn't got rid of him, it's a mystery that some of the lorries, cars or vans he took on, didn't. White vans were the favourites, I suppose because they were driven at such great speed, and speed was the challenge: and that which was doing it needed to be controlled – according to him, I imagine.

The roundabout at the town's war memorial was a great spot, because here you had traffic coming at you from all directions, which really tested your herding skills.

Whether, at some time or other he had been hit by one of these metallic sheep, I am not sure; or maybe he was just getting a bit older, and needed to calculate his tactics a little more accurately. But as time went on he spent more time lying at the side of the main roads assessing the traffic, than actually chasing it. Although this meant he had less chance of getting killed, it nevertheless did cause traffic problems, especially on one occasion, at a rather busy time of day, when a friend spotted him crouching there waiting to take a run at some unsuspecting lorry. Seeing the danger, the friend managed to stop the traffic in both directions while he attempted to drag Bryn away from this high powered game; he had been indulging in. By the time the dog had been persuaded to come away, the traffic was stretching back both ways as far as the eye could see.

Gradually, over the years, we have in some way or other managed to largely cure him of this dicing with death pastime; even so, he will still, on the odd occasion have a go, if he thinks he is sufficiently far away, when you are walking up the lane.

The last memory of this was when a big objectionable BMW 4x4. (The sort that the posers of this life seem to manage to afford), swept by at speed, in the usual bad mannered way some of the more inconsiderate motorists pass pedestrians. Obviously sensing my disgust – perhaps the shaking fist may have had something to do with it – Bryn took him on: and the last I saw of the pair of them - (forever, I thought, as far as Bryn was concerned), was as they disappeared off at speed round the next bend. The dog grabbing at the rear tyre, while at the same time, trying to balance himself between the road and the steep bank rising at the side. Leaves and twigs flying after them, as his snatching mouth attempted to tear tyre from wheel and the scrabbling feet fought to grip the loose surface of the bank.

Thankfully, after a tense few moments, the lad came chasing back round the bend towards me again. His wild prick ears flattened down against his head in all their aerodynamic splendour; his large red tongue hanging from his mouth, dripping heated exhaustion, and the wide grin of "mission accomplished" all over his face – "How about that Dad? That got rid of him, didn't it?" And I think it must have, because I haven't seen the wretched man since!

It was increasingly, at times like this that it became more and more apparent to me, how relieved I was becoming to see him back again. Up until the age of about four, I really didn't much care if he survived or didn't, so weary were we of this animal, but, as time went by, a bond was beginning to form between us; the battle of wills was receding, and it wasn't me who was the one giving in. I was realising by now that to get the dog to respond, I didn't always need to shout at him; in fact, quite often that had the opposite effect. Instead, a quiet reasoning word would bring the right result: and the reward of praise too, was a triumphant and satisfying state for both of us.

Until the four-year benchmark, if Bryn had been out all day with us; we would come home expecting him to collapse into his basket happy, contented, tired, and ready for a good deep sleep. There was none of it; the fact that he had spent the day being active meant he could now spend the following night being the same. The spring in his body had been tensioned by the day's activities – a bit like a toy giro car – when the faster you spin the wheels, the further it would go when released. It was the same when we went out in the car. Motorways were top; they were the places where his excitement and thrills found their peak. The faster we went, the better he enjoyed the experience.

Our two boys tell me: "you are a typical old-Volvo-driver Dad" – and I think to myself. "Well, if that dog behaves like this at 60 mph – I would hate to be in the same car with him at anything more. To watch him through the rear mirror, standing right at the back of the car, was like looking at the determination and concentration on the face of the tillerman, doing white water rafting, except our dog had to keep an eye out as well, for the endless streams of escaping "sheep", whizzing by on either side.

Unbeknown to him, it must have been the loving nature of the beast, which over the first four years of his life had saved him from certain death by my hand. In fact, I knew that was absolutely the reason. Because, I don't think a week went by when I didn't plan in my mind a visit to the vet's for the "final solution"; and then, only to find, in my imagination, the picture of my journey home again without him – How could I have ever lived with that?

By now I was acutely aware of this mysterious closeness growing between us, but my constant reminder of this state would be, whenever I happened to glance round at him, I would find his eyes pinned on me with deep intensity; or to wonder where he had wandered off when there was no sign of him, only to find that he was so close behind me that I hadn't noticed.

So there we are, six years after what might have turned out to be a tragic fatal visit to the shepherd of Worcestershire, to collect the apprentice for the "best little Fella a fella could want," and wondering all the time: how this new little fella would measure up to the old one.

Our minds couldn't even begin to bring comparisons between them, because to begin with, the new was so wide of the mark from the old. Maybe that was for the best; for it never entered our heads to attempt to compare them: only to try to somehow mould this wild thing into some sort of sem-blance of a dog. – A dog; that was all we wanted – a trained cattle dog, had at one time, become just a hopeless figment of our imagination – something we would never be able to achieve from this pest.

Even so, that hopeless figment, had by some mysterious, unfathomable way, become the reality. Today, although the overwhelming power, I know, is still lurking there, just beneath the surface, and does occasionally attempt to break out. Between us, we are almost in control; and the little rebel-lious horror of the past, has become a great chum and helper. (Not perfect, mind you, for I sometimes still need to shout – but full of promise just the same). I have at times seen him chase cattle with such intense vigour to bring them to heel; and then, to be able to respond to my command for a change of direction with such immediacy, that the poor lad has cast himself to the ground in all his momentum.

And more and more I find myself saying to him –
You're another, "Best little Fella a fella could want."

CHAPTER 14

Who Told You Farming Was All Roses Round The Door and Featherbedding?

"I couldn't bring one of my heifers over to you for B&B for a few days to run with your bull, could I – can't get the blooming animal in calf with AI," Sidney Clack was on the phone. This was the third time he had tried to get his heifer in calf, and she was bulling again.

"Yes, that's OK." I replied, "but how will you get her here, my trailer's out at the moment?"

"We could borrow the Lloyd-Baker's horse box – I'll give them a ring, and get back to you." And he did – within a few minutes.

"If you can do it today the horse box is in their yard, take the old one – not the new one," he insisted.

I had an hour to spare so I set off straightaway; and sure enough, when I arrived, in the yard the two boxes were standing there, side by side: both "Rice" trailers – top of the range;

but one looking decidedly worse for wear: and the other –
brand spanking new.

As I reversed up to the old one, Mr Lloyd-Baker happened
to be coming across the yard.

"I'll give you a hand with that if you like" he offered. –
Having studied the trailer hitch for a few moments, and being
rather puzzled by it, for it was quite different from ours, I was
rather glad of the offer, and between us we lifted the trailer
draw bar onto the car hitch.

"Is that all?" I asked – "Nothing else to do?"

"No", he replied, "that's it", and confidently walked on his
way.

"Well, I suppose he must know his own trailers; and perhaps when you buy quality everything just happens for you,
not like the run-of-the-mill stock trailers which we were used
to." I thought, momentarily forgetting at the time that it was
she who ran the farm, whilst he was otherwise preoccupied
with running his own business.

So off I flew with the trailer, despite its age, gliding along
behind me. What a treat this was, to tow something which
seemed to run on silk instead of the jogging and jerking of our
own trailer: and the faster I went, the smoother it rode. – I
raced up the hill towards Sydney's place, as I had never gone
before – just like the wind. When I got to the top I turned
smartly onto his track, winding down the twisting and uneven
surface, and riding over the potholes as if they weren't there.

Just after bouncing down a dip in the track, at the same
time as sweeping round a left-hand bend, my attention was
drawn to a cracking and smashing noise coming from the
bushes on my right. Peering through them, as I travelled swiftly along, I noticed a large dark green structure overtaking me.
Not being aware of any road running parallel with Sydney's
track, I glanced in my mirror, and was able to look right back
along the track over which I had just come, which meant I was
no longer being followed by the trailer: and which also meant
we hadn't hitched the thing on properly after all. So that the

combined lowering of the back of the car down a dip, and the bend in the track had allowed it to break free from me.

Fortunately the crashing and banging, now well ahead of me by now, eventually stopped. So we quickly got the thing back, unscathed to where it belonged, at the rear of the car, screwed the hitch down this time: loaded up the heifer, and cleared off home, before anyone noticed that anything had got out of control.

I always remember that trip with the smooth-running box whenever I go past Sydney Clack's place; and just thank my lucky stars that the trailer didn't get away from me on the hill, or worse still, with the heifer in it, rather than on that track.

It wasn't all in vain either. After a couple of days I took the heifer back; done and dusted: and nine months later out popped a nice little black calf.

Of course we all have a still born calf at some time or other, or even one that lives for a while, and just dies – which generally means there must have been a problem we weren't aware of – genetic or otherwise. ("One of those things", is the vet's usual diagnosis) – I prefer to think of it as one of those things they haven't discovered yet. Although, of course, I would never say that – might upset them.

"Got room in your freezer for a calf" Sydney was standing at the Redworth's door with a black polythene bag full of bits, which he had just chopped and cut up from one of those sorts of calves (skinned first though).

"I thought it would be alright for Boss," he added (Boss being his "deaf" untrainable Welsh Collie), who Sydney was quite happy to forgive for those shortcomings in exchange for his companionship and company, as he didn't have anyone else much inclined to share his long days with, other than the livestock about the place. Not that anyone would have wanted to share her life with him; or him hers I imagine. Even the poor long suffering lady who once rashly offered to keep his new mobile home clean for him, had to give up eventually out of sheer desperation, when he repeatedly managed to sack the place in one day, after each of her weekly – all day clearing and cleaning marathons.

Once you had read the daily papers you chucked them on the floor, it helped keep the carpets clean from your muddy boots, and hid those bills that kept coming. Although that sort of thing did have a downside too, because, not always was he able to get to the phone before it stopped ringing – even if he was canny enough to detect quickly where amongst the piles of rubbish the sound was coming from, for generally it was then that he had to set about digging the thing out.

Fortunately for Sydney, he had a very kind and obliging stepmother who used to visit him on occasions. She, of course, always stayed at the local pub. Nevertheless, because he suffered from arthritis quite badly, he was always glad of extra help and company, and she felt pleased to offer it. It was on one of her visits that the poor unsuspecting woman was sent off by Sydney round to the Redworth's where she was to ask for "a nice piece of that veal which Sydney brought round the other day for you to put into your freezer – We're going to have it for our supper tonight."

Foxes are very often shocking pests, and can cause terrible damage during lambing time, even coming into the sheds and taking the young lambs from under their mothers' noses. Although, thank goodness this is often the exception rather than rule. Outside – lambing is more vulnerable to this type of attack, and once a fox has got into the habit of visiting a particular place, and is successful at making a kill, he will be back again and again.

The same, of course goes for poultry; and it was Sydney, who one winter was suffering badly from a severe spat of those night after night attacks.

Somehow or other a fox was finding his way into one of the deep litter houses, and every morning poor Sydney was faced with the same sight of terrible devastation and carnage – dead birds, torn to bits, headless corpses scattered around everywhere; and those who were fortunate enough to escape the

mass slaughter, were scared out of their wits, and went completely off lay for weeks. Despite the shocking hullabaloo,
which must have come forth from the shed, when the dead of
night visitor arrived, Sydney unfortunately never woke up.

For days he tried in vain to discover where the crafty butch-
er was getting in. Doors were always securely fastened and
padlocked; the walls were built of stone, and there was no sign
at all of anything having burrowed under them. There were no
windows in the walls, only perspex roof lights in the asbestos
sheeting – and that was where he eventually discovered he was
vulnerable.

Tucked away, in a corner was a gap between the wall and
the roof: a gap hardly big enough for a cat to squeeze through;
but there was evidence all around it that something had been
coming and going on a regular basis. As soon as the hole had
been blocked, the invasions stopped.

Until Sydney was fortunate enough to have managed to
buy a brand new mobile home/bungalow, with the help of
family; he had been living for years in a rapidly deteriorating
pile; which had started life, I think, before the war, as a 12 ft
touring caravan.

Fortunately, or unfortunately, for him; depending on how
attached he thought he had become to his old home, the
Environmental Health Dept. of the local authority had come
along and condemned it. – I still wonder what they would, or
could have done if Sydney's brother had not come to the rescue with the new mobile home. – After all, if he couldn't live
on the place, who would look after his cattle and poultry?
Especially as there had been, camping for years, not far up the
road from him, a merry band of system riders, (politely or
P.C. known as travellers), without any interference from anyone, and living quite unmolested without any trace of fresh
water or sewerage pipes – both of which Sydney had – and his
properly connected too.

During the lengthy altercation which followed the environmental snoop's first appearance, amongst many other things a

lack of fire extinguishers was mentioned. So what business was it of his if Sydney accidentally set himself on fire, because he didn't happen to have a fire extinguisher handy at the time? And, has this creepy leach from the local authority managed to shut down that lot up the road for the same reason? The answer to that question was "no"; when I phoned them to ask. The official line was that my friend Sydney was classed as a permanent site; and the shower up the road was defined as temporary; and accordingly to E.H., there lay the difference – Solution – "Speak to your MP and get the law changed"– end of story – life is not that long. Because, here we are ten years later, and those useless twits up in London are still floundering about trying to find ways to sort out these lazy layabouts.

Before the new caravan, and shortly after the battle of the fox, Sydney was embroiled in another very nasty night-time experience.

Safely tucked up in his damp bed, he was suddenly woken in the early hours by something falling onto him from above. Lying there in the quietness of his "bedroom", he listened, and gradually became aware that he wasn't any longer in there by himself. – Something was crawling round the floor. What or who it was, he was unsure, but whoever it was, it was certainly alive and moving, and if he didn't take some sort of action, he could well be a goner at the hands of this intruder.

As his eyes became accustomed to the dim moonlight, he recognised a shape, slowly and deliberately moving across the floor. Quietly he stretched under the bed for one of his heavy boots, and with a sudden leap, and enormous strength, gathered from, he knew not where, he struck a mighty blow at the dark form – and then another – and another; in quick succession: and blow after blow was delivered – until, exhausted, he collapsed back onto the bed.

During the next few minutes he began to recover his breath, and reaching for the light switch, prepared himself for what he was about to see lying motionless on the floor. If it had been an intruder, he was convinced he must have killed him by the severity of those blows, and he himself would probably have been lucky to have escaped with his own life, if he had failed in this attack.

As the light flashed on and filled the untidy caravan with its brightness, Sydney looked at the floor where his last blow had struck.

Lying there in a pool of blood, his coat stained and disheveled: his head thrown back, with the last thoughts of this life – surprise and disbelief, registering on his face was – a fox.

I am not sure whether Sydney ever got over the events of that night. Beating something to death somehow seems particularly cruel to me, as I am sure, in hindsight, it must have seemed to him too; but at the time, no doubt Sydney thought he was fighting for his life.

Over the years Sydney's arthritis grew steadily worse, and at last he agreed to go into hospital for a replacement hip joint. The problem was – how would the place run without him? The answer was eventually developed with the help of friends, neighbours, and his loyal stepmother. They would all muck in, and with Hugh, his live-in workman to do the heavy work, they should get by. – For "live-in" read nice Woolaway bungalow, remembering where the boss lived and for "workman" – read doubtful. In actual fact – Hugh – I felt was only there to give Sydney moral support: to call upon in emergencies; and to draw his wage packet each week. The thing he excelled in best was the wage packet bit.

Size and weight were never on Hugh's side, although about 5ft 4ins tall, he must have been pretty close to that in width too, with the result that he was never a fast mover; so between the waddling slowness of his gait, and the constant bouts of sitting down to get his breath, the days passed faster than the work achieved. Even so, he always had a ready smile on his ruddy round face when he greeted you, and watching them falling about amongst their infirmities with Sydney giving orders, and him ignoring them; turning the simplest job into the most complicated fiasco was always entertaining, provided neither noticed you watching; but I suppose, each deserved the other. After all, who would employ Hugh? Whether he was ever a workable force in his youth, I never knew. But as the years rolled by, some of them must have rolled off onto him too, and you wondered how much more he would expand before he either burst, or floated away like an enormous balloon, with his rasping high pitched Gloucestershire brogue still arguing back at Sydney's barking instructions.

Should this happen, I don't suppose Sydney would ever notice what was going on, or even realise that Hugh had floated off somewhere else. That is, until Hugh's equally large sister came looking for him for his tea. Which according to Sydney was where all their troubles lay. "Too much sweet stuff – always filling themselves with too much sweet stuff." He used to storm.

So it would only be the likes of poor old Hugh who would tolerate the peculiarities of Sydney, and Sydney would be the only one to tolerate the slowness of Hugh. Each then had to take the other as he found him: for they seemed to have no other choice.

The forced removal of Sydney for his long-thought-about operation was an opportunity, I think his stepmother had been waiting for for some time. No sooner had he been swept away to hospital, than she swept and cleared after him, everything he had been accumulating over the years. A mammoth job, even though it was to be just confined to his living quarters. But what a treasure trove it turned out to be.

Most of Sydney's eggs he sold on an egg round, mainly for cash, and because his book-keeping was a non event. Each year his poor accountant was presented, always at the last minute, with an enormous pile of scruffy bits of assorted paper, passing off as receipts, or indecipherable scribblings in his shaky arthritic hand. No one, not even he, knew what was going on. The balancing of these accounts, I think, resembled more a conjuring trick than a mathematical calculation. So between them: the Inland Revenue and the Customs and Excise (VAT) threw endless threatening letters at him: letters which worried poor old Sydney more than all the other problems of his livestock-keeping put together. But because of this great aversion to paper, and his difficulty in putting anything on it, there was nothing he could do, only hope that his long suffering accountant managed to keep the wolves at bay.

Turning up at court, when things had been neglected for too long, for even this magician to spirit away, was an enormous ordeal which Sydney should never have been put through. Although the strange and unfamiliar experience of being taken into Bristol, and then questioned in the court room, for a man who normally travelled no more than 8 miles from his home, never dampened his spirit.

"We'll fight'em in the woods of Ozleworth" was his favourite battle cry. "em" included the VAT, Inland Revenue, MAFF, local government, civil servants and Brussels – in fact anyone who made life difficult for us out here while at the same time, living off our backs – the bureaucrats – public enemy no. 1. And I would say Amen, Amen to that.

Because, like many struggling small farmers, Sydney appeared to live off fresh-air: frugal. - Not a word you hear much about these days of instant everything and affluence. – So, if the money wasn't there – then you couldn't spend it, and you would get by anyway; and if some of the £1 notes and fivers had accidentally slipped down between the mattress and the caravan wall, and some had been dropped on the floor, and been scuffed about a bit amongst the discarded newspapers, and lost from sight, then Sydney would be the last person to miss them – and if you never had, then you never missed. – Never had – That was until his stepmother started discovering crumpled and dirty bits of paper of regular sizes and shapes, turning up between the layers of deep litter in the caravan.

Only after the first two or three armfuls of rubbish did she notice what was going on, when a few of these notes fluttered to the ground, and from then on it was a long and laborious process of sifting through every single sheet of newspaper, spreading them out, and examining front and back for anything that might be clinging to the damp surfaces. Every day too, she flattened out the mucky notes as best she could, and trotted off to the local building society, where upon after about the third visit they began to complain bitterly about all the filthy lucre she kept turning up with.

During the detailed investigations, which were turning more into a treasure hunt than a clearing exercise, with all the added excitement and sense of adventure, the heavy mattress was dragged eagerly from its place against the caravan wall. I imagine it was then that she must have been brought up short, at the unbelievably squalid conditions her stepson chose to live in. For the weight of the mattress was nothing to do with its quality, but more the amount of water it had absorbed over the years. Just the same, if that was where Sydney was happy, then there was nothing she could do about it.

Animals and birds, like people don't go on forever, so when a batch of laying hens reaches the end of their useful commercial life, they are despatched and turned into chicken paste or pies. Nothing wrong with that, they've had a good time scratching and fussing around amongst their mates, in a dry, comfortable shed, protected from the elements, with food and clean water provided.

Alas though, all good things do come to an end eventually, and after they're all packed off on the undertakers lorry, it is quite strange walking into a poultry house, where you are normally greeted in the morning at feeding time, with an ever increasing crescendo of excited voices, all singing the same cackling song. Or perhaps like an all female crowd at a football match might sound, I think.

So when the chicken house is empty and silent, and very lifeless, it seems that its heart has been taken from it, and it is no longer a living thing: full of little ginger feathery figures all scuttling about their daily business. It is then that the long process of mucking out the litter, brushing down the roofs and walls, removing and scrubbing the perches and nest boxes, and disinfecting the whole lot ready for the next batch of young incumbents all turned neatly out in their nice red fresh feathers, like children in their new uniforms, on the first day at school.

Extra help would be needed on those occasions at Sydney's, and the old faithfuls generally could be relied upon to turn out.

The tractor: (when new and spanking red, courtesy of a legacy left by Sydney's mother. - There was after all no other way of recapitalising the place, only to hope that things lasted long enough for the next relative to come to the rescue by dying). The tractor and trailer, reversed into the shed, and from then on, was the end of the mechanised bit. – It was forks and shovels, and hard graft after that. Needless to say, Hugh was always seconded to feeding and collecting the eggs in the other laying houses, (light work).

Once everything had been cleared out and cleaned, the job of disinfecting and bringing back in the perches and nest boxes began. Disinfecting was an important job, which Sydney always insisted on doing himself – not only because it was important and needed to be done thoroughly, but because it was relatively easy; just wandering about the place with a garden sprayer full of Jeyes Fluid, sending the remaining cob-webs jetting off into oblivion, and feeling good about all the hygiene.

The trouble was, the enthusiasm for the job often overtook the operator: and staff, as well as equipment were sometimes given the treatment. Jeyes fluid in your eyes is always bound to give you instant, but I think, not permanent blindness; and it was poor old Tony Redworth's turn to come in for it.

Spluttering and groping and falling about; the effects must have seemed like germ warfare. Only the cursing and swearing would have confirmed that Tony was far from dying.

"Sorry Tony," shouted Sydney, "you must have walked into

it." Knowing that sort of remark would normally have provoked Tony to even more anger; but he knew he was safe here today, because Tony had more to be thinking about than slating back off at Sydney.

"Go into the bathroom and wash your eyes out in the basin," Sydney kindly suggested, realising that he had gone a bit too far by blaming Tony for his carelessness.

A 12-ft pre-war touring caravan doesn't generally come fully equipped, so things are not sometimes the way they sound. Bathrooms and kitchens take room, so if your touring caravan is not going touring anymore, why not put your bathroom in a shed somewhere, and put your kitchen in another shed somewhere else? So with two little self-contained corrugated iron sheds to choose from, somewhere about the vicinity of Sydney's caravan, Tony set off, arms outstretched, hoping to arrive where he was supposed to.

Happy that he would soon sort himself out, the remaining workers set about bringing the perches and nest boxes into the poultry house, but keeping half an eye out for the exterminators garden syringe.

Within a space of a few minutes, the happy smooth running of the operation was once more interrupted by a loud bellow. Again, it was Tony's voice; but this time, instead of being raised in anger, it was a cry of disbelief and horror.

Yes, he had arrived at the right little shed – Yes, he had managed to find the wash basin – and the tap – and yes, the fresh cold water had soothed his eyes as he lent over the basin to swill them; and which allowed him to slowly open them without that stinging sensation.

But – "No!" – What on earth was this in the basin barely 1/2 inch from his nose. Two dead and almost completely decomposed chickens, heaving with thousands of white fleshy maggots, as if they were just about to drop the lot onto the floor, and walk out with them through the door.

By the time Tony appeared in the doorway of the poultry shed, still spluttering from his experience, everyone had stopped work again, wondering what all the fuss was about this time.

As he spat out his revelations in the bathroom to the gaping faces – Sydney quickly took over, got the thing back under his control: and with his usual matter-of-fact voice, reserved for these occasions, said, as he turned his back and continued his hygienic sprayings – "Oh dash – I meant to pluck and dress those two for dinner last week!"

If a chap wanted to sell eggs from his poultry himself, instead of through an egg packer, it meant he would need to grade them into different sizes, and pick out all the cracked ones (or seconds, as they were known in the trade). These, at one time, you could then sell to people who weren't fussy about a bit of dirt, cracks, blood, and the odd embryo, which you sometimes got if the poultryman was stupid enough to run a cockerel with a flock of hens, as some of those half ignorant, half clever good-lifers thought you had to. The thinking was, I imagine, that if you didn't have a cockerel amongst all these females, you wouldn't get eggs either.

Eventually, after Edwina Currie, when she was some sort of health minister in the Thatcher government, uttered these famous words: "Sadly, most of the country's hens are infected with salmonella," and succeeded in destroying the whole of the United Kingdom's egg industry in one sentence – and, at the same time, thank goodness, destroyed herself in the process. (of course, the silly woman had got it completely wrong, but the damage was done, and it took years for us to recover from it). From then on, you weren't allowed to sell a second quality egg, and they all had to go for pasteurising into the confectionery trade.

Nevertheless, before the salmonella hysteria, followed closely by B.S.E. hysteria, had set in, and people valued food for its true worth, and didn't have all these stupid hang-ups, stoked by dodgy scientists, promoting half-baked, untested theories in their quest for notoriety and the odd MBE; cracked eggs were good value, with a ready market, and

Sydney Clack should have, and meant to, exploit it. But he missed the boat; and cocked the job up, as usual. Because instead of promoting those wonderful value goods, he just let them stack up on egg trays inside the door of his grading room, gathering dust, and whatever else happened to be flying about.

No doubt if anyone wanted to buy cracked eggs, he just took the tray on the top of the stack, leaving the rest sitting there amongst their ageing mates. I reckon, the stack, from about the 3 ft level down was anything from 4 months to 2 years old, with Sydney always promising himself to get down to the job of selling them. Something I was rather glad he never did, because if he had, it would have created the most almighty epidemic of food poisoning throughout the district that anyone would have ever experienced. But worse still, Edwina Currie would have probably got her job back, because the daft twerps would have thought she was right after all.

Sydney's egg grading room was really another shed tacked onto the end of the poultry houses, and would have been of adequate size for the job if he hadn't - like he did with his living quarters and delivery van - filled the thing up with rubbish, mostly old egg trays or, if the post or newspaper happened to come while he was in there grading eggs, with letters, bills and newspapers as well.

The result of all this untidiness was, if you visited him in his egg room, you had to stand outside because there was no space inside for him and you, which meant you held your conversations standing either side of the door. I never liked doing this much, not because I was stuck outside (although, if it was wet it wasn't very good), but because it meant I had to watch his egg grader working.

Normally, a small single-operator grader like he had would keep you very busy, putting the eggs on at one end, and taking the graded eggs off, and putting them on trays, or into boxes at the other. Sydney's was different from this. I think it must have gone wrong once, and he probably got someone to repair it for him as a favour, using cogs they found lying about. The result was a bit like clouds drifting across the sky on a windless day, but Sydney seemed quite happy with its performance. I suppose it gave him time to do other things while he waited for the eggs to amble across the machine.

There was a short period, during the time when we kept poultry, that I bought Sydney's eggs, and we graded and packed them to sell on our retail vans. Generally I would call into his place and pick them up in our estate car. I think, as far as I remember, if you packed the car right, and stacked the eggs on trays loose (not boxed), up to the roof, and filled every corner, (the load space with the rear seats folded down was about 7 ft long), you could squeeze in around eight thousand eggs. The theory was, that if the stacks of eggs were packed close together, they would travel as one mass, giving them greater stability, and of course it would be much quicker to load the car this way, rather than waste time packing the eggs into 30 dozen boxes at Sydney's end, only to have to turn round and unpack them again at the other.

What you had to remember though was once you were moving, you were not to stop again too suddenly or swerve too violently.

There was a bit of an artist, who used to live round here, and drove about in a Morris Minor van. I haven't seen him lately – so he's either moved away, been banned from driving, or killed himself. I think the latter is the most likely, because, on this particular day, if I hadn't swerved up onto the grass verge, he would have killed himself then and there, (or me, I suppose). As it was, he got away with it, and the last I saw of him was in my rear view mirror, belting round the next bend as fast as he had come round the previous one, where I met him – head on.

Milk and blood is the same, when spilt makes one heck of a mess – and you think, if it's blood, "If someone doesn't do something quick, I'll bleed to death."

Eggs are like that too. Once out of their shells they develop

192

minds – The yellow yolks go skidding about on their whites as if they were alive; sliding off down the tiniest crevices between the plastic pieces of bodywork. Underneath the floor mats, soaking the carpets, dripping down the back of the seats, and lying in great swirling yellow pools on the swabs with their broken shells bobbing about like miniature boats. Even if you're sitting in the seat at the time, they still find their way down between it and you, and you end up practically floating in a sticky glutinous mass, where it then begins to slowly soak through your clothes, and the ones that didn't stop at the back of the seat, did, at the back of your head, where they managed to smash themselves up and leak off down your neck.

The others, that had more momentum whizzed over your head, ending up in the footwell, where they started filling your shoes.

That morning, I think I lost about a quarter of the load, and I spent the next couple of days stripping out as much of the car as would come, and every piece of plastic and every bit of seat which I removed, had egg behind it. For years, until the car was eventually scrapped, whenever the weather was damp, the smell of liquid egg seeped from the bodywork, like a ghost from the past.

CHAPTER 15

We're Not Really In Control, Are We?

"Well, the prices are definitely an improvement on previous years, I reckon we could now send a couple of our bulling heifers for the next year's sale," I said turning to Pat, as we walked back to the car, after spending the day at the pedigree sale in Abergavenny Market.

"Not a bad sale, and I'm sure our beasts measure up pretty well to most of those there today," I added.

Ever since the B.S.E. fiasco back in the 1980s – 1990s, when some hidden away scientist, by the name of Richard Lacey, a "so-called" microbiologist working at Leeds university decided, that because he THOUGHT, (but has never proved, even years later), that a disease in sheep known as scrapie had jumped the species barrier and caused B.S.E. in cattle; and then THOUGHT that B.S.E. in cattle had jumped the species barrier again, and produced what they were then calling new variant CJD in humans, (still never proved, even years later); the cattle trade has been devastated.

The effect of those half-baked theories, which this forgotten laboratory hack had on the media, was unbelievable. He, of course, broadcast it as proven fact, which incensed the farming fraternity so much that there was serious talk of dragging the wretched man through the courts. A course of action, which was later abandoned because no one had yet been conclusively able to produce the evidence to prove anything to the contrary. (After all, how do you prove a negative?)

At last; years later things are beginning to improve, and the epidemic of n.v. C.J.D., which the "experts" had been predicting has still not happened, and there appears to be a lot of those people now beginning to change their story, and keeping their heads well and truly, firmly down. I only hope that Lacey and I are still about when the balloon does finally go up; and that this man, will at last be seen to have been talking out of the back of his head.

So at last, confidence was beginning to return to the pedigree breeding cattle sale rings, some 15 years after B.S.E. was first discovered.

Anyway, here we were, as we walked from the market on a lovely September afternoon, clutching this tiny glimmer of hope, that after BSE and foot and mouth, things might now return to normality; and that good pedigree breeding stock would once again be sold for the purpose for which they were bred – To proliferate the good name of the best British livestock, instead of simply being sent down the road to the nearest abattoir, and ending up on the nation's dinner table – But don't hold your breath, because if this municipal, urban government doesn't hurry up and get off its backside pretty smartish, and deal, in a balanced way with disease in wildlife as it does with those self-same diseases in cattle, the next farming horror story is going to be TB

So another year began and the cattle diseases of the past paled into insignificance, with the discovery in my dear Pat of the greatest and most feared of human diseases rearing its ugly head. We had never reckoned on anything like this when we began the journey through the new year, and it was something we were glad we hadn't foreseen. But life is like that, isn't it? How easy it would be to go demented with worry, if we knew what the future held for us. As it is, with modern medicine we can only pray, and hope that what for about 8 months changed how our lives ran, will now be behind us. Although the honesty and realism of the medics is always there at the back of our minds. "Well, if it is going to come back, it will within the next 5 years": was the straight answer to our straight question.

So life goes on and we picked up the ball, and we are running with it – And Pat? – Well, she's great – she's best at it.

However, the year rolled on and we were soon back to another September again, and were looking forward to testing our belief that breeding cattle prices were lifting. We had booked in two of our 2-year-old heifers for the Abergavenny sale, and the catalogue having arrived, were busy studying the competition.

Eventually the morning of the sale came: I'm not a believer in prettying up stock with shampoo and fuss, I think, a beast, provided it is clean should be seen as it is.

The two we were taking were from the same line, Cwm Parc Awen 6th and Cwm Parc Awen 7th. They had been penned up early that morning, and left to settle down before being loaded into the trailer. Having checked the paperwork, (DEFRA – the new face of MAFF – but the same old bureaucratic bunglers, with hardly a pair of Wellington boots between that lot in Whitehall) know where all the cattle in the country are, and their ages, and their sex – That is more than our government knows about us humans, remembering the thousands who turn up on our shores every year, and disappear into the mist.

With the trailer ramp down, and the gates in place, it was now a simple matter of coaxing the two of them in.

The trouble with our livestock is that they are all born and

bred on the place; they always stay outside, winter and summer, and they never go anywhere unless they walk there. Even
so, always, eventually, after gentle persuasion with soft words,
they do go into the trailer – Patience and tactics are the two
things we have to remember.

"She's going to be a problem this one," I remarked to Pat,
although I needn't have: anyone could see she was going to be
a problem. Awen 7th it was, slightly longer in the leg than
Awen 6th, but she was the boss, and she didn't want to go in,
and she wasn't going to let the other go in either: shoving her
back with her head whenever Awen 6th attempted to go onto
the ramp.

After half an hour of gentle coaxing and soft words, we
resorted to a couple of sticks, which made no difference at all.
Every time we pushed her forward, she would spin round and
make for the back of the pen, where I had to promptly get
myself; placed between her and the gate to the field. On about
the 5th attempt to beat me to this spot, and failing; she had
obviously had enough, and whether I was standing there or
not, this time she was going, and she did, - straight for me she
came, and as I side stepped – over the gate she went.

Cows are generally not the best jumpers, but as long as they
can get their front halves over a gate, they seem quite happy.
Because with their mid-drifts straddled across the top rail of
a gate, their front legs firmly on the ground at the other side,
and their rear legs flaying about in the air – they know that we
can never lift them back again, but with a bit of jerking and
wiggling, they are soon off, leaving behind a couple of frus-
trated outmanoeuvred twerps; and a bent gate.

All over the country, as you travel about, you will come
across bent gates. A bent gate is generally caused by an escaping cow, and has always a sagging top rail; those are the tubular steel sort – the wooden ones you don't see because they
generally get completely wrecked.

"Well, it's no good, we can't waste any more time trying to
get her back; we will just have to go with the one," I moaned.

So we turned our attention to Awen 6th, who, after a few quiet words from us, obligingly walked up the ramp and in, and off we set, an hour late.

"Not the highest figure I had in my mind, but I'm happy," was my verdict to Pat, as we walked away from the sale ring. "Worth coming back next year, but I will certainly be expecting more then the way things are going; it's all showing a lot more promise now; let's hope it stays that way" I added. "And the other?" she asked, "What will you do about her?" "I might ring the chap who bought this one; but on the other hand, we could get a phone call from someone at the sale, who would be wondering what had happened to the second beast." I said.

"What happened to the other one then? Came the Welsh woman's voice over the phone; after we had been in the house about an hour.

"No point in beating about the bush" I thought – "Escaped" I retorted.

"Like that was it?" came the reply.

"Well, not really, normally she's very placid, she must have been spooked by the trailer." I came back.

"Is she like the other?" was the next question.

"Identical, except she's a bit longer in the leg" I said.

"I'm interested. Can we come and see her; do you think she will load? Was the thousand-dollar question. "There will be three of us," she added.

"Well, we'll stand a much better chance then," I responded, feeling happier.

"How about Wednesday afternoon – 3 o'clock?" "We are coming from Llandeilo, so it should take us about three hours", came the reply.

Pretty well on the dot they appeared.

"I haven't penned her up, so you'll be able to see her better," I said, with as much confidence as I could muster, thinking to myself that she had better go into the pen when we need her to without any fuss; or we're really sunk.

The Welsh woman and her husband, followed by their

daughter, studied closely the object of their interest, walking round the animal as she stood considerately for them in the field. I'm not sure who was studying who the closest though, the beast or the people. Cattle are great suckers for routine (like all animals I suppose), so as soon as there is a break from it, suspicions and some recent memories are alerted, and of course, this one had some recent memories, which you could see, had just become alerted, and which was why she was starting to fidget and move about, generally in the direction away from the visiting party.

"I like her, and she moves well; she's equally as good as the other one. What will you take for her?"

"The same as the other," I said, which I thought was fair – "That is the price I get after all the auctioneers deductions," I added.

"That will take her down below £500." She came back; which shook me. "I might as well send her to the abattoir if that's the case," I said: for I knew her calculations were based on a wishful myth.

"Don't let's argue about the figures, if you'll have her, when I get the cheque from the auctioneer, I will ring you, and you can send me a cheque for the same amount. You could always phone the auctioneer and confirm the price." I said firmly, (at least I think it sounded firmly anyway).

"That's fair," she said, "but I think I'll pay you £300 now to show good faith, because you don't know anything about us" she added. Which was quite true; although I had taken the trouble to check them out in the breed society's herd book before they had arrived; and they were breeders of long standing, so I thought I was on fairly safe ground.

Having agreed, the next job was to get the animal into the pen ready to load. Fortunately, after hiding the purchasers from sight behind a hedge (because strangers are often trouble in the eyes of stock). Armed with a length of dead electric fence wire, with Pat at one end and me at the other, we approached Awen, and the nearest beast to her, and swept them both into the pen with hardly a pause.

There are two things to remember here, one is, never expect to get a beast anywhere away from the rest by itself. You would be extremely fortunate if you succeeded, for they are, after all, creatures with a very strong herding instinct, so you always need to take another one for company. The other is, that only you know, (that is, if your stock have been trained to respect an electric fence) if the wire is on or off – they can't tell by looking at it – and neither can you, come to that. But if you saw a couple of people walking about with a length of electric fence wire, you could be pretty sure it wasn't on. That is where we have the edge on the stock, because, they think electric fence wire is always on, and accordingly, move away from it.

Instilled with this new confidence of getting Awen where we wanted to, with no trouble; and to allow her to settle down; we all decided to adjourn to the kitchen for a cup of tea, and complete the paperwork.

Half an hour later we all emerged again, me having pock-eted the £300 cheque, and the woman from Wales having hand-bagged the paperwork.

The trailer was reversed up to the open gate of the pen, and everyone was strategically placed to close in when the beasts approached the trailer ramp. The trick here is to take two animals up to the trailer, and at the last minute, when the one you want is just about to go inside, you turn the other back, and niftly shut up the ramp, shutting in the correct beast. – That is in a perfect world – What you do if the wrong one goes in, leaving the right one out, is to start all over again; after about the third time of this happening and both animals beginning to get wound up, the one you want thinks that enough is enough, jumps the gate, and leaves behind five frus-trated and outmanoeuvred twerps and another bent gate.

Whether it is that the Welsh are patient and triers, or whether it was that just these three were, or perhaps this shrewd woman from Wales knew a bargain and a good heifer when she saw one and was determined to get it, I don't know. Anyway, whatever it was that drove them on to attempt this same exercise of re-penning, and re-loading the beast three times, didn't come off. Because after the third breakout, another hour and a half later and 10 ft. of the wooden pen smashed to bits, we still found ourselves in the pen, and the object of the exercise, once again outside, and heading off, this time, at speed to the other end of the field.

Remarkably, as they prepared to drive off on their 3 hour journey back to Wales with their empty trailer, she having hand-bagged the £300 cheque, and me having pocketed the paperwork, they still managed a smile, leaving behind them those infamous, and always consoling agricultural words: - "Well, it was just one of those things!"

After agreeing to think about the situation and try to decide on new tactics, a week later we spoke again on the phone, but even after considering all the options, we could find no satis- factory way of dealing with the problem. So the deal was off. Which left us with an unloadable animal. A bit like those blokes who we describe as unemployable, I suppose. Someone has spent years rearing them, only to find, in the end, they have turned out to be useless. What's the good of feeding an animal, and spending money on it, to find too, in the end, you can't get the thing off the place, so that someone will pay you money for it?

"You don't happen to know anyone who's got a couple of heifers for sale, do you?"

It was about one week after the abortive loading attempts; and the voice on the other end of the phone was that of the National Trust's local warden, who was responsible for all their cattle in the area. "Welsh pedigree, of course" he added.

"Yes, we've got just one, would that be any good?"

After he said it would be, I set forth to tell him of the long saga we had just endured.

"Can I come over and see her, and take it from there", he replied. – So he did. – He liked her and said he would have her at the price I had agreed with the Welsh woman.

There are people who say they like a challenge. I can never quite understand whether they're serious, showing off, or a bit stupid.

You don't need to like a challenge, or try to create a situation where you get a challenge, because sooner or later one will come along, and there won't be anything much you can do about it, other than take the wretched thing on, or stick your head in a hole, and hope it has gone away by the time you take it out again.

Having got this beast on the place with some sort of birthright, and allowed it to stay here while we reared it, seems to have given it the feeling that it has now acquired a sitting tenancy: and has the right to refuse to leave. Thank goodness though, we will be able to deal with its obstructiveness in our own way, instead of trailing off through the courts, as we would if she were human. Nevertheless, one can't help wondering for how long will this be the case. No doubt there will be an animal rights lunatic working away at that somewhere or other, to soon get it changed.

So here we have this so-called challenge. A buyer willing to pay money for an article we are having difficulty in delivering – At least, we now have a buyer.

"Leave her with me for a couple of weeks, and I reckon she will be persuaded," I said to the warden; having by now had that last week to think about it, and to realise that it would be not just a matter of man-power but plain and simple tactics which would win the day in the end. He agreed, and went off, expecting to collect his purchase in two weeks' time.

During the period that followed, instead of feeding Awen her hay with the other beasts, we gave it to her, with a mate, in the pen, next to the feeder which the other cattle fed from. After a few days of this special treatment, the two of them were always waiting to be fed each morning at the gate of the pen, which was by now associated with food, not the trailer.

At the far end of the pen was a cattle crush, which was used to restrain beasts if they needed to be treated for anything. Here the hay was placed next, and here she was enticed to stand, quite happily, even when the gate was closed against her, holding her exactly where we wanted.

The end of the two-week period was now fast approaching. Remembering that she was a bit of a jumper, the sides of the pen were raised an extra 2 ft using spare gates, and a date and time was fixed with the warden, who would bring along with him the girl from the farm down the road for extra support.

Having a detailed plan fixed in my mind for the final and most delicate part of the operation, we now had to put it into practice.

Gently the warden's trailer was reversed up to the crush gate, behind which Awen 7 was standing, the same gate, which each day, she had been let out from after finishing her hay, and from where she could join the other cattle. The trailer ramp was quietly lowered, and the side gates to the ramp securely tied with baler twine to stop her pushing them back and escaping, when the crush gate was opened for her release. All the other cattle outside the pen were gathered about the trailer by using an electric fence, and where Awen could easily see them. Her mate was still in the pen beside her, but on the other side of the crush rails; this meant that when the time came for loading, we would not have to try to separate the mate from her, but would simply try to persuade her to walk into the trailer; an exercise we had now attempted no fewer than a dozen times – and failed.

"So what's the difference?" I thought, as we went off up to the house for our cup of coffee, to do the paperwork, and allow her to settle down before the final and most tricky part of the strike. – Well, for a start I had got a sedative from the vet, which wouldn't knock her out, but just make her more amenable, (worth a try if you had a stroppy wife, I suppose). Although the vet's parting words, as I walked from the surgery were: "I'm not making any promises mind;" which didn't exactly instil confidence in the stuff.

Whatever we do, nothing is foolproof or guaranteed, and this was no exception. Animals, like people are not always predictable and we did have a couple of weak spots in this system. If she took it into her head, she could jump the side gates on the trailer ramp, which couldn't be heightened if they were to close easily, even though two of us would be lurking out of sight with sticks if she attempted to have a go, and could jump into action and try and knock her back - always remembering though, how this had failed in the past. The other weak spot would be when the crush gate opened; she might simply refuse to walk out into the trailer and, knowing how stubborn she had been before, that was a distinct possibility.

So with the coffee drunk and the writing writ, we returned to her which we hoped to outwit.

Everyone quietly took up their positions, two secreted away on either side of the trailer, and a back up, in case they should need it, and with me now ready to give a quick movement, and fling open the crush gate.

When we had all finished nodding to each other to indicate that we were ready, I quietly, but swiftly sprang into action – jerking the lever which thrust open the crush gate, whereupon she, just as swiftly, sprang out of the crush – onto the ramp – and into the trailer.

No sooner was she in, than the four of us dived for the ramp gates, releasing the baler twine, and closing them across the back of the trailer, into which she had just disappeared – I half expecting all the time that she would reappear on her way back out again – but everything was safe and secure, with the ramp slammed shut: she just stood where she had landed, quietly surveying all the action.

For several minutes I just leant on the gate, not able to move for relief, disbelief and mental exhaustion. Or perhaps I was maybe waiting for her to re-appear; bursting out through the metal sides of the trailer – the conquered, once again unconquered - but nothing happened, all remained absolutely still and silent: she had surrendered, and by the way she was standing peacefully in there – had been quite happy to do so.

That was October, and during the following few months Awen 7th settled down without any trouble, amongst the National Trust herd, loading whenever she needed to be moved, without so much as a murmur.

Except – One morning in February the following year, out on one of the Trust's high commons, and after a wild night with violent winds and torrential rain – the warden discovered her standing with the other cattle, contentedly cudding, but accompanied by a delightful little heifer calf, all cleaned up and fed, and enjoying this new found world of hers.

"But she shouldn't have been in calf" I exclaimed when he phoned me.

"Are you sure it's her calf?" I said in disbelief.

"Yes – no doubt at all," he replied, obviously very happy, (thank goodness) to have this unexpected bonus.

The remainder of the day was largely taken up with me wondering and pondering over this seeming virgin birth. The problem, I was feeling was that I wasn't in control any longer. I didn't even know when a heifer, who hadn't been near a bull, had somehow got herself in calf – The stuff couldn't have blown in the wind, could it? Something like the experience Pat had when she was training as a young midwife. They had before them an unmarried girl who had just produced, and was busy trying to convince them that she must have picked it up off the lavatory seat in the public toilets.

In the end, I turned up something in last year's diary, which could possibly be construed as the answer.

During the May of that year, we had taken a couple of days away in Brixham. I say a couple of days. We left, after I looked at the cattle in the morning of the first day, and returned on the third day, looking at them again that afternoon: and on both occasions everything had been perfectly normal. This, then just left day two, when I hadn't seen them; and must have been the day the blighter came on bulling, jumped two electric fences to get with him; and after the dirty deed was done, jumped the two electric fences back again, and we had been none the wiser, and I bet, all the time the pair of them had been chuckling to themselves, knowing how they had successfully managed to deceive us when our backs were turned.

Well, our couple of days away weren't meant to be a dirty weekend, but it looks as though they managed one. Although, they didn't reckon on being found out nine months later, did they?

CHAPTER 16

So Why Do You Do This?

This is the question I get asked by other people, and the question I ask myself probably more than any other - So why do you do this? The simple answer, without putting too much thought into it would be - "I don't know". But if, when I think more, I might just about make a case, which some, even then, might not fully understand.

I suppose why people farm is one of the great mysteries of life; the return is so very poor, especially for the small or part time stock farmer who has to take his business seriously, because he relies on it to pay his bills, unlike the hobbyist who is doing it purely for pleasure, although even he falls by the wayside sometimes. It is risky - that goes without saying. At times, those who practise it feel quite inferior because this is the way we are often treated by so many of the well fed, nannied people who think the countryside is their own personal playground, to be kept in a romantic, pretty state by some peasant or other from the pages of our history books. Who, because he is able to work and live in constant bliss, in a summer landscape, where the sun shines gently down on him from morn till eve, should sacrifice the means of getting a fair return for his labours.

That's right isn't it? I have that about right? Hopefully, for those who have read this book, they might not feel quite that way, and are by now more enlightened. Although I could go on ad infinitum about all the other things which haven't been included in these pages, such as the weather, the endless paper and red tape; and many more sad and worrying tales which are often lurking about for those of us who keep livestock.

Nevertheless, whatever your occupation, there is always a downside, but at the same time, there are many compensations too, and farming has a few. How to put them into words is another matter. Some middle-aged farmers would probably say they continued to farm because it was a bit late now to do anything else; others would find it extremely difficult to adapt to any other life style. Some are tenants so they would lose their homes if they quit. How would others get from their beds in the morning, if, instead of going out to tend living creatures, they went off instead to a factory or office, and spent their day with inanimate objects, such as machinery or computers?

It is one thing too, to visit the countryside as a spectator, for that is as close as many of us ever get to it, and quite another to be part of that countryside. To help fashion and shape it, to work with it and for it, and to be an intrinsic part of it. Not to be looking in, but to be looking out. To know the trees in your fields, and hedges and the livestock who shelter under them. A place where you are not just passing through, but are staying for as long as you are allowed, that is. It is home, where home is not just a place, a house, a small sheltered spot where the things you need each day are gathered about you. It is a home where life, which stretches away, way beyond even your own boundaries, is a part. The point where you stand in a familiar place and gaze at all that lies about you, it is that sort of home. The place where you know more of its characteristics than any other person; the folds in the hills, the wet places, those that are hard and stony, where a tree in the wood fell years before, or a foxes den or a badgers sett, hidden away from the casual visitor.

The livestock you care for each day who share this home of yours, and are part of it. Those who you have known for years, the old cow who has always, without fail, produced a calf, for you and she to share in rearing; who is as gentle as a lamb all the year round, but who, when she has her new born calf beside her, is as dangerous as a lion, towards even you. Each cow, some young some older, are as individual as any human, in character, in temperament, in their likes and dislikes, or their looks; whether in their face or figure. The calves, right from an early age develop their characters very quickly. The twins, who are always together, whether grazing out on the hillside, waiting for their feed on a winter's morning, or standing round the hay feeder. And as they get older, the heifers especially, take on the looks of their mothers; the dished face, or the Roman nose; the high tail, or the big ears. All are known to you as no one else knows them; and you are known to them, as they know no other. And you share this place with them - this place which God has created, and you have borrowed and cared for, just as long as your will, or health, or circumstances, or life will allow.

The closest people to you, who will often wonder themselves why they do this, are other stock keepers. Those to whom you have most in common; who face the same problems, and share the same joys. Who each morning go out, come wind, storm, blizzard, or iron gripped frost to tend their charges, but who also can share in the happiness of a new born lamb or a calf; and the first flush in the spring, of the brilliantly emerald grass on a hillside. To have the camaraderie of these people, when you can sometimes go off and visit them in the isolation of their homes, down a remote valley, or up a rough track to a crumbling little hill farm. To share with them some of the unspoilt splendour of God's creation. To stand at the top of a mountain, where the sky stretches itself away before, above, around and beyond you, casting its ever changing face of shadows and softness, or darkness and gloom; or simply its clear and brilliant azure. Where the huge patterned landscape below, on every side, tumbles and falls over itself in its rush to display the beauty of its endless diversity, with wooded tumps, rocky slopes, tree shaded soft fields, surrounded about by their bouldered boundaries. The snaking river glistening its quiet gentle way, on the last few miles of its long journey from remote mountains to the glorious sea.

All this perhaps, will help explain a little of why we do this. It is something unique, it is something which no other person can quite imitate, or will be able to stand where you do, and share in its secrets.

Of course some of this, or all, despite how you feel, can, when there is change, be taken from you. After all, life is transient; our animals have but a fleeting life compared to ours; and our lives are so temporary compared with even the trees in the wood. And the forces from without can steal away from you these things which you hold so dear; and powerful government can be a great destroyer of that which it does not fully understand; because men are merely men, whoever they are; and are so often inclined to make disastrous mistakes in their crusade for a cause.

Whether it will be something such as this which will, one day drive, or make me come away from it all; or whether it will be my choice or no choice, none of us knows; only that, whatever it will be, if I am still able to reason, I know I will feel sad, so very very sad; but at the same time; glad, so very very glad to have known and played a small part, and to have done this.